Poet of Truth

Volume 1

Poet of Truth

My Web Site:

https://poetoftruth.wordpress.com/

Poet of Truth Volume 1: Poet of Truth

Table of content

Introduction

With devil may care flourish, I branched out into the cyber world to express my opinions in prose form. Here for the first time, collected into one book, grouped by themes and hopefully, will allow the reader to follow along with my way of viewing the world. I started out as a poet, and while it may not seem as obvious, the connection is in the language. There are three forms of written or spoken language. Ordinary, such as you may speak with your friends. Technical, which is like your mechanic or doctor may speak. It sounds like a language but unless you have the secrets of their mean, it really is simply too technical. The last of our three is the grouping of Religious, political and poetic. High words of ideas that embrace the eternal, or call upon it for meaning, to be brought from the forums of Plato into the world of man and allow our minds to be unshackled from the tyranny of mindless amusement into something much deeper then the score of last night's game. From out of The Cave in to the light to see what shall ring hallow and what shall ring true. I hope this work, that I have created, will help you touch on to my eternal truth, my poetic truth.

1. Climate

Climate Change

Let's talk about climate change!

Why screams the hecklers...

Why not?

As in why I am not into the whole climate change thing in the first place.

First, those who do not believe in climate change are called "Deniers". They take that term from Holocaust deniers. This is a very overt Ad Homonym attack. If we look back upon the beginnings of Quantum Mechanics, today responsible for so many things like GPS and Quantum Computers, The great Albert Einstein would have been called a "Denier". Yet true scientists of the time, like Niels Bohr, Erwin Schrödinger and his cat, instead of crying foul, took up the challenge presented by such opposition and worked harder to perfect their theory. Never once did they whine, cry or moan. They worked harder to prove their case. Not assume that there mere utterance should be accepted as utterances from the Heavens. So why do they in the climate change camp need to do take such an unscientific stance to begin with? After all, as Al Gore said; "The science is settled!" In fact, science is never settled. Isaac Newton's Theory of Gravity was published nearly 400 years ago and is known to be wrong. Einstein (such much denial from this man) had to re-write Gravity 100 years ago. Yet for all Newton's version being wrong, NASA was still able to land men on the moon using it. But at no time was it every considered settled, not by Newton, not by Einstein and certainly not by NASA. So why the rush AL Gore? What's with the personal attacks on those who disagree? Science is never about either, personal attacks or religious dogma? Yet for some reason Global Warming is about both. In a similar vein, we are told that the majority of scientists believe that Global Warming is to be the true facts in this case. Really?

Well, see, at one UN conference, on a Sunday night as delegates rushed to take their planes home, a vote on the matter was called. Of those members who remained, a majority of them voted that way. This sounds to be as biased as you can get to wait to call a vote so late in the conference. Those who stayed until the end can be seen as having a reason to remain, creating a sampling error in the vote. Those that voted having a reason to give a yes vote into a higher percentage. Science is about careful consideration. Not a rush to judgment by people with false agendas. Science is the clash of idea, not name calling. And finally, science is the about unbiased consideration of the evidence, not merely who can rig the vote.

NASA says that this past April was the warmest month of April on record. That sounds scary, but is it? Our record keeping is bad, in fact, very bad. Today we use sophisticated measuring devices. But 140 years ago they looked outside for record keeping and wrote colder today. Not as rigorous as we might like. As well, the places where we measured those temperatures were once outside of the city limits to prevent and protect from micro environmental factors warming their readings. Now the cities have grown around those same locations and they give out readings that show warmer. There seems to be another explanation here than global warming. The other point to discuss is; what does climate change mean? Yesterday, was warmer then the day before and today is warmer still. See Global warmer is proven! Except, not so fast, that sort of evidence is not considered by any side to be evidence of anything, let alone global warming. The reason is, too small a period to measure and say anything meaningful about. What if this was true from months, then years and then decades? Just what is the period needed to say anything with certainty. Alas, we have no answer. Would we dare call it climate change? Recall to mind that in the 1970tys, climate scientists were saying the world is cooling. Wonder how that theory worked out? But yes they scream we now have better models. In fact, scientists do have better models over the last 40 years. And they have better measuring equipment. What they don't have is any sort of agreement on the size of sample, should they use; a day, a year, 40 years, 400 years, 4000 years? All unknown and uncertain. And in case you missed this point, they only have data of questionable veracity going back 140 years. Ice Core, Tree samples and other sampling methods are of limited value for the global expression, merely recording the local events over time. Then we can look at the computer models they use. These are based on large dimensions of the atmosphere, usually measured in square miles. They would need to have it at the level of square feet, preferable to the leve3l of square inches. This is like watching a very small bit video on a much large screen. The result is pixilation. Large blocks of square things fill in the picture as the video codex tries to make the picture larger without adequate information. It might work on the tiny level; it won't work in the big leagues.

The whole Meta notion of climate change and global warming are red flags to a bull in a china shop. It enrages the community and draws out less then useful discussions. People simply do not believe in the whole idea because they have been turned off by the heavy handedness, overzealous, holier than thou approach. Instead of trying to form consensus and educate people, the entire approach by climate change advocates has been to threaten people; "a majority of scientist agree," insult; "deniers", or belittle; "The science is settled," and allow for no meaningful debate when the basic facts are not agreed upon yet.

Now, back to reality. I think we all can agree that when a forest fire burns, you put it out. When a ship spill oil, you clean it up. In the middle of the Pacific Ocean is a mass of plastic, the size of Texas. I suspect that no one has studied what this does to the weather not to mention fish and sea life, but can we not agree that it needs to be cleaned up? How about this, we need to lower car emissions to prevent smog in cities. Not we need to lower car emission because they cause green house gas. Nope, we only need to agree so far on this matter to help keep the air clean in our city. No need to poison the well and go that extra mile to say climate change. For we do not need to involve that sort of speculation, Occam's razor can be used here and still lower the toxic gas we have to breathe. Another example is the many proposed pipelines stretching from Canada to the Gulf of Mexico. Many environmental groups oppose this pipeline. As do I. But must I oppose it solely on environmental grounds? Or is this a big tent and we can all work against the idea without having to agree on why it should be stopped? Do I have to convert and drink the cool aid? Or can I say I oppose this idea for economic reasons without commenting on the environmental factors?

For all these reasons and many more, I will not agree with anyone that climate change is occurring. How it has been presented to the public, and whether or not it is even science, let along proven fact or "settled."

Feel free to call me a denier if you like, but don't make the mistake of calling yourself a scientist, or that you are doing science. It is all propaganda when you resort to insults proving what a weak argument you have indeed.

Carbon Tax

Here is a simply idea that governments are going to make too complicated. We have a carbon problem, which may or may not be the case. We have a solution; we tax carbon emitters, such as factories and cars. We cap their level of carbon they can emit and then lower each year. If they surpass they have to buy credit from someone else or pay more taxes on it. Those that reduce more are able to get a credit for their reduction of carbon and sell it to others who have not. Sound great except where again does this help us now? So we have less carbon in future. What about removing carbon from the world now?

They have not let us down, they have an idea. They will capture carbon and store it deep underground in aquifers to hold carbon. Never mind, just a few problems, like all that construction, or what if it leaks or just how much energy would it take to capture the carbon in the first place to store it under ground. Both ideas are bound to not work, and mostly cause more problems than they need to.

We need to capture carbon? Assuming this is true, how about we go old school on this. You know full retro, all the way back to nature. Yes, nature. What is the best carbon capture means we have? Plants and trees. Take a car using gas. It releases so much carbon per km. This is easy to test. Then figure out how much carbon a tree will use to grow over time. Compare how many trees are needed to absorb the gasoline released carbon into the air. Add in the cost to plant those trees, the purchase of land and the general in efficiency of government generally and you have a real carbon tax. That not only will beautify the world, trees grow into forests, and in future we can harvest those trees to reuse that captured carbon in a sustainable process. The best part is this, the tree start to absorb the carbon in the air now, as they are planted, so no hopefully future plan that will have to kick in, many, many years down the road. The cap and trade will simply be abused, go ask Volkswagen for their real environmental impact and compare to what they programmed their cars to report. The carbon storage is wasteful in additional energy and resources, not to mention the carbon is then lost and not reused.

Fort McMurray

As Fort McMurray burns from an out of control wild fire, forcing the evacuation of some ninety thousand people, fleeing here and there to escape the inferno, is it now time to address Global Warming? In fact, I think it is a very bad time to get into that whole kettle of dead, smelly, stinky fish. For a number of reasons, first, Al Gore claimed that "The science is settled." on this end of the world apocalypse as we know it theory. In fact, at no point is any piece of science ever settled. But just like one does not swear in a church, bring up such a contentious issue has a better time and place then over the smolder ruins of what used to be a city. The problem being is that Global Warming is not a strictly speaking scientific debate. It has no real standards to compare itself to or what measure to go by. All science is based on study of events in repetition. So I drop the ball and measure it. I do this a thousand times I can measure the acceleration of gravity. Global Warming is a singular event, happening right now. Scientist point to previous events that may show similarities to our modern event, but over what length or period time do we compare it with, how many years, century, or millennium, do we compare this present period with or to? For example, it seems to me that winter is coming about a month later and November and December are not as cold as they used to be. April is frightfully cold the last few years, at least 3 or 4 of them. Is this my subjective view point, or will time passing bear out a shifting of our seasons? Did I detect climate change? Or is that just another example of uncertainty on what time period or term we can use in our understanding of climate change? No agreement on any definition, boundary or timeline exists in the literature even from the scientists who claim Global Warming to be fact. Yet Fort McMurray continues to burn into the long cold night.

On the other side of this debate are the irrationalists; who claim that science is nothing, evolution is not even a theory and that the only work to be trusted is the Bible. They discount the global warming claims not for valid scientific reasons but because they don't understand anything to do with the scientific method. (Do not pat yourself on the back if you do support the Global Warming hypotheses, you have Al Gore and his religious view of the settled science involved.) Thus we have two distinct sides with strong differences and yet strangely enough, Fort McMurray continues to burn with neither side offering us any solution or even a way to help those unfortunate victims. To which I say, they are both wrong, we need a new third alternative. In the middle of the Pacific Ocean lies a mass of plastic bottles the size of Texas that by 2050 is expect to grow so that there will be one bottle for every fish in the seas. For all the global warming debate, can we not agree that somehow this is not a good thing and that someone should clean up this mess? Stop adding to this mess, and find a lasting solution to this mess? We can start by agreeing that this is a mess that something needs to be done to fix it.

In the case of Fort McMurray, the cause of this fire; be it a lightning strike or a dropped cigarette, a camp fire not extinguished properly, the cause is not global warming. It is human. The disaster is compound not by climate change, but by a city government that allowed for a river to act as their only fire break, thinking the roaring flames will never jump over the cool water, until they did in May of 2016. See, I don't need to call upon God to accept responsibility for this disaster. Nor do I need to scream Global Warming or Climate change as if the fault could be so easily assigned. No, the problem is human error and only humans can fix it. A fire break would cost the city money. So much money that they cannot afford it...

How much will it cost to rebuild the whole city after fire destroyed it? I am betting that it would have been cheaper to have a fire break. Just a guess mind you, but I stand behind it. I am also betting that the new city will have a fire break and the budget to maintain it each year. Thus I say to you, we need not accept the religious element of either side. I don't know and I don't care if Global Warming had anything to do with this, I do know that Fort McMurray continues to burn and someone has to put that fire out. Abstract theories need not apply. So for the bottom line, Climate Change or Global Warming or its polar opposite the deniers need to both step aside, they are doing no good.   Not knowing the answer to some abstract *Cause Belli* won't put out the fire at Fort McMurray, nor will they pick up an empty plastic bottle. We will put out the fire there, not to prevent Global Warming but to save communities. We pick up the plastic bottle not because leaving it causes Climate Change but because we may need to drink that water, or eat of the fish that live in that ocean. The third path is to have real reasons, to deal with real issues to find real solutions. Leave the abstract world to its own eternal debate. Grab a water hose and help fight the real fire.

But I am countered by the notion that if we could find the cause of the dry weather then we could eliminate the problems altogether. To which I say, that this is silly. Fort McMurray burns by human error in protecting the city with a large enough fire breaks. Forest fires will happen no matter what you think about the science of climate. They will not stop even if we had a complete picture of the environmental change which we at present do not have. The question is to make sure Fort McMurray's disaster won't happen again. I can get near universal agreement on making the next city have fire breaks that are larger and more effective. I cannot find any agreement on Climate change, nor upon what to do about it. More study is needed to find a smoking gun. No study is needed to see we have to protect out cities with better security, fire breaks and political will to make sure they are respected.

Water ship Drown?

In the environmental front, we have protests over the continuing need for pipelines to transport oil and gas. Simply put, a pipeline make economic sense as it involves no humans to carry the liquid from place to place. So simple and easy. Except, the pipeline breaks and this causes problems of spilled oil. Well there is a simply idea to solve both concerns. The people building any new or future pipeline must agree to a new law. And the law is simple, any environmental damage clean up will ignore the corporate veil such that any front corporations and executives are liable until such amount as the cost to repair and restore the damage is paid for. This way creating front corporations to protect against liabilities, from spills and clean up will be forced up the food chain to the people who are profiting from the pipeline itself, including directors, CEO and all listed managers will be liable for all damages. The next pipeline to be made will have those assurances built into them. I guarantee you that once this new law is passed there will never be another pipeline built because no matter how they lie about pipeline safety, the people who will suffer are not only those who are directly affected by the spill, but everyone connected to it. Under those conditions, oil and gas will return to being transported the safe way.

Global Warming

NASA has declared that August 2016 is the hottest month ever recorded, making it the 11 month in a row where the temperature of the world has increased, breaking old records and setting new records. What more need we say to prove Global Warming. How many more months before you admit the end of times is here, death, dying, gloom and doom. Yet those nasty deniers continue to spew their lies and deny the heat of hell's doorway, as it flash flames the world.

Or we can try and look at the matter scientifically.

First, let's make a comparison to each month being one second. So for the last 11 seconds the whole world has been heating up. By what measure do we compare this to? Minutes? Hours? Days, weeks or even months? Let along years decades or centuries. Global weather records perhaps at best go back 150 years or so. Using these comparisons of months in seconds, we are talking about 11 seconds out of the last 30 minutes. But even that is an invalid example. For what NASA is telling us is not the local weather or the weather for whole country or even the average temperature at surface. Using satellites, they have gathered the temperature for the entire planet as best they can observe, from the temperature in the oceans, to the air temperature at all elevations and into the Atmosphere and stratosphere. Record the whole temperature at all these locations to boil down to one single average temperature for the planet. They do not get into the scientific certainty factor of this, or how tiny the number is in the difference. They don't need to. Any increase is telling. Fine. But now we are comparing apples to oranges. NASA does not even have records of global temperatures much more beyond 40 years ago at the outside. So instead of talking in our comparison about the last half hour, we are talking about the last 4 minutes. And in the last 4 minutes of this analogy, 11 seconds were the hottest of them on record. Great. This then proves all things to all scientists so we can thusly deduce global warming is real? Are you seriously expecting this to be seen as evidence of the whole analogous day?

Sadly, no. It just say's we are heating up over the short term time span of the last few years, beyond which record are meaningless, going beyond the evidence that we actually have on hand and frankly unscientific because we have no basic agreement on what it might mean or any theories to explain it so. There are many things we need to do for the environment. False science of Global warming is not one of them. Fight for reason science, real environmental protection and real battles for our planet. Not this hyperbole of rhetoric. There is an ocean of plastic in the Pacific the size of Texas. Clean that up would make a lot more sense than crying wolf with global warming. No one is buying it any more.

Climate Change Math

Sir Francis Bacon claimed that for any science to be worthy of the name, it needs to be mathematical. As such, Darwin was only a naturalist until George Mendel and his pea plants discovered genetics and inheritance. Until he discovered E=MC^2, Einstein was just a guy working in a Swiss patent office. So for all the claims that Climate change is scientific, I ask them for a simply and seemingly easy answer. Show us the math. How many tons of carbon pollution over what time period will result in what increase in the global temperature? Seemingly, this is something that should be as easy to show as F=MA? And until you can, then I would suggest that the Al Gore's and other pundits of the world not say that the science is settled, for it is clearly not.

2. To be Elect

Clinton Verses Trump

In order to qualify this election, we have created a list of best to worst results that we can expect. Note this is not the best possible results, as that would require Bernie Sanders to still be in the race and win the presidency. As that will not happen, we have to face reality and that means Clinton or Trump. The two most hate politicians in the records of polling such questions.

Best Clinton wins and Democrats win both the House and Senate. In which case for the next two years they might, just might get something done in the passing of progressive legislation. They might fill in their nominations for the courts and they may stumble on some good policies to help working and the poor.

Next, Clinton wins but they lose the house to Republicans but win the Senate. This means the Iran deal is safe but little will get done. Paul Ryan is but a shadow of real leaders in the House, where what the speaker would say would become law. Now his speakership is merely cardboard cut out they use to toss rotted fruits at.

Next Clinton wins the Presidency and loses both House and Senate. What might likely occur? This result will means four and possible eight more years of ideological gridlock and posturing. Little would be done and even less would be accomplished.

Last, we turn to a Trump wins, in any combination of victories in the House or in the Senate. He does not know how to rule, how to work with, or how to create anything. The man is a shyster as can be seen in his so called "Trump University scam." At this point despite the incompetence at the top, the transition team will find good people if ideologically bent to take up the offices in Washington and may even figure out a way to work with Tea Party enthusiasts to get something worked out. For example, Money out of politics would be nice. But I won't hold my breath. Four years of trump, will the republic still be standing? For surely it is greater in its summation and grandeur then even he can destroy... not that he won't try his best to do so.

Real Issue with the Debate

Hilary Clinton seems to be destined to win the Democratic Party's nomination. Where she will then be out-classed and out-flanked by Donald J Trump. This classic definition of hubris shows that even though Bernie Sanders is in the lead over Trump in national polls and would win the election if the poll numbers hold up, she will not let him do so. For her very own Greek Tragedy is not to be denied. This is her last chance to be the first female in the oval office, come hell or high water she is going to beg, borrow and steal every vote she can. Sadly, voters everywhere know it and will vote accordingly. Yet, one thing is clear, once she fails, like Icarus tumbling from the sky in a flaming trail of feathers and wax, she will turn to cast off any blame upon herself and point her fingers directly at Bernie Sanders for not dropping out of the race long ago. He is the one who has hurt her chances by staying in so long. Except for the simple fact that she is the second most hated politician in the USA with Donald Trump being more hated. Go figure why anyone would want to stay in the race to force real issues into the debate?

The Donald

The top five reasons why Donald J Trump should not be elected President of the United States

1) He is a con artist. From his charity foundation buying a picture of himself, to using other people's money to make donations o the same amount, this foundation was mostly a way in which The Donald could fund rentals for his own businesses. Then there is Trump University where his sales reps, keep pushing people to max out their credit cards for the next big course. All for the student gain of nothing of value, no degree, no job, just an inflated credit card bill. If he was really that rich, he would not be stealing pennies from the poor house.

2) Treatment of the press: The Donald has been doing all he can to destroy the power of the press, from isolating hem into a set area where he can pick on them at his rallies, to merely attacking them as biased in his speeches. What little respect people have for the news will soon be lost. The Donald would go even further as President, so much for the 1st amendment.

3) Treatment of women: "Grab them by the Pussy" is now a mainstream legal word that the FCC won't be fining Howard Stern for any more. The Donald has made it a mainstream word. Lenny Bruce is somewhere above dancing at this expansion of the words you can say on TV. George Carlin has changed his skit from the seven words you cannot use on TV to 6.

4) Assassination of Clinton or merely the jailing of: What third world fascist government openly calls for assassination or jail of their rival? Small Hand Donald has done both in this election and in more than one form and at more than one time.

5) Rigged elections: Saying the only way he would lose is if the election was rigged, at the same

time as Republicans, desperate to avoid a melt down along both the Senate and House turning to Democratic control, are actively seeking way to disenfranchise as many minorities as they can. What's next revoking the 19 amendment allowing women to vote? Undermining the essence of democracy because he, having failed to win the plurality, is poor sportsmanship and childish.

Any one of these reasons is enough to not vote for him. All of them says vote for someone else.

2016 Elections results, One Word, Family

How I understand Donald Trump and Hilary Clinton. There is a lot of head scratching and wondering as we awake to the world of President Elect Donald Trump. Small hand Donald, "grab'em by the Pussy" sexual assault prone, trice divorced accused rapist will soon have his hands on the button. What button? THE Button, you know that button, hat start World War Three. And yet with all of that, people still voted for him. Why? Why we scream into our nightmares, why, why, why? I think of all the answers put forward, it comes down to family. What? The Donald, has been in more failed marriages, treats women with disrespect, flirts in a lecherous fashion with his daughters (Cause not all fathers are in touch with their feelings enough to be able to say "I love You" to their daughters, so rather than that, they make up comments to tease, bother and annoy. Some outrageous and some rude, but all of them are expressions of love. By all accounts, Donald Trump is a moral degenerate, yet his daughters are not bother by his comments, or bothered by his actions, because they know what he is saying when he says outrageous things to them both in public and in private. Hilary has been married once, never divorced, has a daughter in good standing with the world and plenty of grand children. Shouldn't she be the idea of family itself? Keep it real. The idea is to have that one marriage for life, the kids and grandkids and all that. Except it is some sort of fairy tale. Some fantasy. The real world is filled with broken homes and broken families, where awkward dads make stupid jokes about their daughters trying to find some ground to meet them half way into who they have become when all grown up into maturity. Where in the back rooms, the "boys" make rude jokes about girls, and if overheard, mother would go "tut, tut, tut" as they make the family supper. Where we the guy across the street says "you stink." Them's fighting words and you tell him so. Even in

New York, you get in my face, I get into yours. That is real. There is one in every family, and if you don't know who it would be in your family, it's probably you. And yet, through it all, for the good, not much good if any, the bad and that is really, really bad, and the ugly, let's face it, it does not get much more uglier then Trump's comments. Through all this, one thing stands out, the guy is family and that makes all the difference. Hilary for all her ability and smarts and social stability, is unapproachable. Not real and not family. She is a winner, she won the family lotto, she won the job lotto, and she is the exception. Not the rule. Donald Trump has screwed up more business then you can imagine, because he is literally stupid. And yet so has that one guy in the family. All in told, this emphasis on family might sway one out of a hundred voters to vote Trump's way and that is what he won by. The horrible, rude, imbecile or the Miss "I am too perfect to believe?" Who would you vote for? Americans voted Family by about 1% ahead of Clinton where it counted.

As Nero Fiddled, Rome Burned

Now, while Trump tweets, Washington is in flames?

Are we in fact watching the decline and fall of the American Empire? Is the United States of America in its final divide? "A house divided cannot stand," said Abraham Lincoln, who managed to survive the Civil war. Today, will that same house outlast the cynical partisan divide? Have the house Republicans out distanced any sense of balance, fair play and dived into Hubris that they simply don't care what Donald Trump says, i.e. The Bowling Green massacre, The Sweden massacre, the alternative facts, The Obama wire tapping. And the list goes on. Yet at the same time we have Mike Flynn resigning for lying to people about his contact with the Russian ambassador, Jeff Session perjuring himself over the same question to the Senate and multiple people popping up to say they too meet with Russians during and after the election. Is Donald Trump's administration merely the new Russian front? And what about the sex tape that they Steel file claims is out there of Donald Trump peeing on a bed Obama may have used, all in the best spy footage ever taking by the Russian KGB latest installment as FSB, Federal Security service? And all of this and Trump has been in office for not his 100 days but just over the first 50 days? And just who can forget the inauguration, watched by the largest crowds EVER! EVER! Thus screamed Whitehouse spokesmen Sean Spicer. As he flushed any hope of his having any credibility down the "newspaper wire." Along with his shredded reputation and the truth be flushed, by lying in his first press conference with the media, Spicer tossed any hope that this President would be anything but insanity, greed and ego of a clearly disturbed man in the highest office "You can't handle the Truth", screamed another equally silly little man named Colonel Jessup in "A Few Good Men."

Sadly who ever might remember such an event clearly was not there. America was built in part on the largest internal economy allowing for the free shipment of goods and services within the borders until now, where congress will be asked to pass legislation for 1 trillion dollars in infrastructure renewal, except it won't renew anything. It will in fact, sell off the highways and bridges to private interests creating new tariff walls against this free movement. You cannot get there from here, unless you pay, will soon be the norm.

Thankfully, in the houses and in the streets, Americans are angry, pissed even. Those few who hate Obama care but love the Affordable Care Act will soon realise they are one and the same. Well they will realise it once it is gone, repealed and replaced. The red states who voted for Trump are also the states that need Obama care the very most. Burnt once shy twice? We can only wait and see what will happen in next year's midterm elections. Yet even that is not enough, if the people merely elect blue dog democrats instead of blue dog republicans. They need to find a liberal to rally around. They need to unleash the progressive wing of the party. In short they need to take back the hands of government from those who would drive the country to the brink of disaster. Or surely as the Roman Republic fell, so too will this republic. Not by war and invasion but by greed and stupidity. It is truly time to make America Great again. This starts with the remove of Donald J Trump from Office that he has stained by his mere presence. The removal of his many cabinet picks with competent people and the overthrow of the Republicans death grip on the Congress. The people need to stand up and be counted for. Or truly Washington is burning to the ground to extinguish the shining beacon of hope for freedom and liberty.

Dateline Washington

Still under Russian Control

The Congress personifying the so called Leninist term, that Lenin never used, of being "Useful Idiots" continue to think they are so clever in hiding their actions from the American people of destroying all progressive legislation passed in the Obama years. A useful idiot is someone helping a third party, usually the Soviet Communists, or in today's case Putin's Russia, to destroy the American dream from within. They think they are using Trump and his team where as Russian is using them for their own ends. Paul Ryan, speaker of the House was astonished to understand that insurance was for those not affected by events to help those that were afflicted by such events. You buy flood insurance as a large body in order to protect the few who are flooded in the rains. Ryan's astonishment was based solely on never having seen Ayn Rand use the word in any of her nihilistic ramblings rather than his merely being stupid. Insurance? How dare those sick people pay into a system that would entitle them to help when they were struck down and afflicted with disease? Stupidity was the theme of his presentation to the media on his proposed Trump care. It is one thing that we assume you are an idiot, it is another to open your mouth and prove it to be the case. What is amazing in all this, he is consider to be one of the smart republicans and yet has not a clue what the concept of insurance is supposed to mean, supposed to do and supposed to be there for. The health bill is D.O.A., dead on arrival. The left hate it and so does the right, albeit for very different reasons. So much for "Repeal and Replace." The health care act is merely the tip of the iceberg for the so called right wing trying to undo any and all progressive legislation. What the industrialist money owners want changed is that Obamacare is an additional tax on their greed and need to impoverish all workers from any hope of a long life beside hard work, sweat and toil for their corporate machines. For Trump it is bread and circus. As the small minded run around fighting over the crumbs, he and his small hands are quietly gutting the Department of State, the IRS and any other department they can get rid of. America used to have worldwide influence and some, not much, but some, moral authority in the world at large. No more. And done in with less than a 100 days in office. What a winner he is that small handed guy. The USA has gone from weak leadership under Obama to outright incompetence under Trump, and the only one who does not see it is Donald J. Trump himself. Steve Bannon, his special councillor, think of the movie "The Godfather" for a closer to the real truth portrayed of his job function as "mafia consigliore" to President Donald J Trump. How this man with clear links to right wing extremists is able to sit on the national Security Council boggles the mind. Let along that he is sitting in the same office as the President. His only goal is to remove the USA from the world stage into some neo isolationist camp and let the world fall to pieces. Only to be picked up again by who knows. The wealthy feel they have a puppet as a president, yet are missing the clear comparison to Hitler, who in his day was considered to be an idiot. Was considered to be their puppet and was considered to be under control. Wonder how that worked out for them and the world at large. Not to mention the Jewish populations among other minorities. The sad thing is that Trump has not even tried to hide his displeasure with Mexicans or Muslims, yet when he signs his travel ban people are surprised that he is doing this? The insanity is clear. And no one is going to win, just everyone will be losing.

God save America... because their politicians won't.

Getting the Joke

In President Donald Trump's world, were the grasp on truth is tenuous, alternative facts and outright lies are abundantly clear as being the message, a feature not an occurrence. One is constantly seeing the pundits in the news media question how people can support him. Seemingly, with each day, some new lie, some new scandal, some new revelation that would have derailed another president, is brushed aside for the next tweet, the next press conference, the next thing to send the nagging chorus of bird song to an even greater, higher pitch. From fake massacres, to "Pee-Gate" to sheer laws on the amount of people attending his inauguration, it is day by day insanity. Chicken Little had but to cry once the sky is falling, to awaken the barnyard but by the third, the other animals rolled over and ignored him. This President has not had three times, or even three times three. Nope, not even 300 times 300 times shocked and outraged the world or what should have done so under any other president. So what is going on? What do the 40 percent of the American population not get in their continuing support of Donald Trump?

The answer is depending on who you ask. Trump and the White House don't care about anyone else is opinion. They won. And you don't matter. So to the victor goes the spoils and let the hog feast begin. Some pigs are more equal than others. In the Hour and Senate, they don't care either. In a Republican controlled Congress, they only need some idiot who will sign into law whatever they pass. So it does not matter what is the latest scandal issued from the lying White House, so long as Donald Trump signs whatever is put in front of him, without question, they won't care either.

The last party involved is the people of America, those voters who voted for the man himself. The pundits who think they are all so smart, have no clue what is happening out there. They are told they are less smart, less sophisticated, less informed or else they would have long turned against Donald J Trump. Except, it is impossible to not see all those things. From Saturday Night Live to the internet to network talk shows and Cable new services, all of them are aglow with the merits of everything done by President Trump. So what are the people not getting about this conman shyster in office who is more than likely a Russian agent? We return to the first question, what are these people not getting? The answer is they are getting it, they are getting it all. What the 4th estate is not getting is this. Trump is a clown, and even the dumbest of person can see that but he is upsetting the smug self righteous elite who run the news media. He is causing them to run around like a chicken without a head. As they scurry hither and fro, the media is being mocked in the mockery, they are being laughed at by those in the laugh. The joke is on the media. The good job Donald Trump is doing is not governing the country but in upsetting the media. Drive the frenzy of the 4th estate. Dragging them to the absurd as they try to sound impartial when faced with nothing but childish taunts. Donald J. Trump is doing a fabulous job challenging the professionalism of the journalists of every sort. In that challenge lays the reason he is supported. Over the years, the dumb people, the absurd people, those who the New York Media Elites have turned down their nose to, they became the majority. They control democracy and even if they only won by a hair, it was a fine hair indeed. They won and if they want the clown to entertain them while Rome doeth burn? Then they are the will of the people. Welcome to democracy. Sometimes the good guys don't always win the polls. 3 years and 11 months to go. Get plenty of sleep; there is no sign this is going to slow down any time soon. Bread and circus in the twenty first century, thy name is Trump, all hail (spelled Heil?) to the new President.

Tree of Liberty

A time has come again?

"The tree of liberty must be refreshed from time to time with the blood of patriots and tyrants." -Thomas Jefferson

The power of democracy and the American dream is the myth that all can partake in the feast, all can through hard work and ethical behavior reach for the stars and settle for the planets. However increasingly, the deck is stacked against us. The game is rigged. The odds, always in favour of the house, are seemingly only in favour of the house. When the people demand fairness and accountability, the politicians must be answerable to those calls. Or as we are seeing early in the presidency of Donald J Trump, revolution is abound. In a place where there is one gun for ever man, woman and child, this is no peaceful sentiment. But thus far those in protest are being peaceful. So far. The real rebellion will occur in 2 years if the momentum is conserved across time and distance. If it is, then this will be the first rebellion in history fought not with guns and bombs but with the ballot and a stroke of the pen. The question can only be what is to happen if the elites and business tycoons who own the politicians fail to take heed of the coming storm. Will they brush it aside as they have in the past, ignore the Lilliputians once more and grant themselves even more of the collective wealth by government tax breaks and outright hand outs? Or will the dawn arrive where the rich notice the unsustainability of their constant actions. Where people are burdens by debt for health care, Imprisoned for lifetimes for minor crimes, all because some herb is deemed illegal? Traffic tickets as revenue agents and road piracy targeting out of state visitors travel on highways as a means of seizing cash to fund cash strapped police forces? 240 years ago, the rallying cry of "No taxation without representation" cause the Colonies to take on the world's only super power and win their freedom. Are we seeing that once again the people have found their backs to the wall and are taking action, organizing and prepared to backlash against the republicans and democrats alike, who only favour their rich donors. A president who has more skeletons in his closet that he shares with Putin's Russia and a court system that allows for some social progress but is firmly in the interest of business? Can we see the tide is turning? Can we see a new wind blowing in a wind of change? Or is it, just a new tempest in a tea pot. The last such wind from the right paid for by the Koke brothers, blow in the ill wind of right wing do nothing to help people only help ourselves. Will this new wind blow the dust off the new deal; bring in progressive socialist legislation on health care, taxation, and new amendment to get money out of politics? As of this writing, the next election is some 19 months away. Where in politics a week is an eternity, where will we be then so long into the future? Hopefully, the time will be used to gather money and people. Mobilize a work force dedicated to introducing progressive legislation and enforcing the electoral choices above the whim of the representative. In one insane statistic; Americans overwhelmingly support background checks from the low 80 to a high in the 90 percentiles. Yet, lobbies like the NRA prevent any sort of waiting period at all. And actively resist to the point of targeting people that dare vote in such measures. This is a democracy? This is a Republic? Jefferson was right; it is time to shed some patriot's blood and the blood tyrants upon that tree of liberty, in a death by a million votes, one ballot at a time.

Troika

Donald Trump being elected President, Briexit and the Columbian Peace plan, now if I added all walked into a bar... You would see the joke involved. However three major upsets, some claim defeats of the powers that be and I think all can be traced back to the same cause. Or rather group of causes. In the case of The Donald, people who voted for him were White males above the age of 30 without any education or only some, the hinterland for him, and the cities on the coast against him. The same can be said of Brexit, where the young voted to stay in the EEC, as did Scotland and the big cities like London. The older, rural folks voted to get out. The last of our troika is the peace plan. Again it failed by people who were not in the thick of the fighting. In this case, peace was mostly in the cities, whereas the war was fought in the rural farmlands. The young were also ignored. But there is one last thing to remember for each of these. The turnout was low, lower than expect and lower then needed. Without a clear and overwhelming turnout the voice of the people is drowned out by the voices of the motivated. Most people don't want war. They don't want an economic collapse and they certainly do not want 'The Donald'. Yet they also don't want to vote even more. In the age of wedge politics, where you only need s a small sliver of the pie, 25% who are motivated to vote, the rest will have to fall in line behind those small, vocal voters, whereas the rest of us have to pay that price for their voting behavior.

Briexit

With the Briexit this week in desperation people are resorting to scare tactics to win over undecided voters. Here is one example trying to get people to vote to leave the EU. In a race baiting video on Facebook, Britain First reported that birth rates were declining across Europe. They showed a number of countries include Germany whose reproduction rate was at 1.38. To reproduce your population you need 2.11. What this means is for every female you need to have at least 2 live births, one birth for replacement of each partner, and a little extra to account for illness and early death. Their claim is than that the western world is in decline by this falling birthrate. The Muslims are going to take over Europe and the Hispanics will take over America simply by out producing the so called "Home Team." Coming just days after a Britain First supporter, or someone shouting their slogan, was accused of murdering Jo Cox, A British Labor MP, shows extremely poor timing. The simple fact is this; Britain First should stick with comedy because propaganda is not their thing. The only person who killed Jo Cox did not have an Islamic agenda. Britain First most certainly does have an agenda. The killer of Jo Cox was not shouting out "God is great..." But even within their ramblings we can see this video's failings most clearly. First, they assume all Muslims, of which there are 1.6 to 1.8 billion of them, will act with one will, one voice or even one thought. This is facile to start with but if it were the case, we would already have been overrun. We also the question of reproduction, the fertility numbers used in this video lie on their face as the average for all people means that all people are included, such that the people who arrived yesterday are lumped in with the people who arrive 200 years ago. When you migrate, you assimilate. Those numbers that Britain First used include Muslim and Hispanics and Africans who are coming but also the ones who have already come in. In other words, all this fear and trembling by racists groups like Britain First for their so-called "invasion" by these so-called "Others" are silly, as If the battle of the birth canal was merely the importation of raw demographic numbers from one country to another. Forgetting that the people involved might have something to say about it. They might have something to do about when they learn they have a choice in these matters. Where even if the first generation are longing for their lost land, the next generation and all who come after, call this new land, home, Islamophobia merely shows an irrational hatred of Muslims in this case, or any other groups they don't like. They arrive; they assimilate and disappear into the bed rock of society where they become the newest wave of protectors of the very bedrock they belong to. Think Irish and Italians in the United States, often portrayed as the criminal class such as the Mafia. Yet American law enforcement is filled with both ethnic groups because it is their family tradition. Here are three further examples to show how silly Britain First is; First Germany in the late 1960 and 70s, wave after wave of Turkish Muslims arrived as migrant workers to Germany. They came in with the same high levels of birthing, 8 children per female that BF is using to threaten us with today. And so what happened? By now they should have over run all of Germany. Missed that on the news? What happened is this. They arrived, they assimilated and they became "German." The women stopped having so many babies, they got jobs and education, the same as German women had done before them. And with that they stopped having kids, because women with choices, i.e. not barefoot and pregnant, do not have as many children. The girls do not identify themselves as Turkish. They speak fluent German. Their children are as foreign to Islam as the blond hair blue eyed friend they are playing soccer within the local field. And ironically of all, the birth rate for all of Germany also includes these Muslim immigrants as well. So if these immigrants had kept up the same proliferation, they should have a marked increase in the birthrate? But they did not. Because that is what happens to people when they move; they adopt the ways of their new world, country or city to feel at home in where they live. Not some other place they do not know. Second example; the mayor of London, a Muslin named Sadiq Khan, born in London and educated in that city; same for the mayor of Calgary, Alberta, Naheed Nenshi. Both men are respectively British or Canadian. They are not Muslim then something else. In a similar vein if slightly different, Donald Trump calling out judge Gonzalo Curiel, the man who is presiding over Trump in his legal dispute regarding Trump University, as being a Mexican. This judge was born in American. His parents as well. We have to go back to his grandparents to see who last lived in Mexico. His family has been American longer then Trump's own family. Yet he is the Mexican who is biased according to Trump. Our last example; when the offices of Charlie Hebdo were attacked, the first police officer on the scene, there to restore order, protect the innocent and arrest the guilty, was brutally slaughtered by the gunmen for the uniform he wore, because he was one of their so called "oppressors", of their so called "Islamic revolution". Definition of a hero is someone who runs towards gunfire instead of away from it. This man, this hero, his name was Ahmed Merabet. He was 42 years old and he was a Muslim. Thus in the most ironic twist of fate, a so called Muslim coward killed a real Muslim hero on that day in front of the office of Charlie Hebdo. Isn't that interesting, the people we are told to fear, are the ones who ran to their death trying to rescue us outside those offices. Remember that the next time you hear the words "Je Suis Charlie"

Just like the successive waves of Eastern Europeans, Irish, and Hispanics to the shores of the USA, just as they have previously done and so too will others continue to do. People will move around this world and will assimilate into the culture of where they live. They will in fact become embodiments of that culture. They will change it and be change by it, making it a living breathing thing that belongs to them as well as to the other people. This lack of live birth shows government needs to produce more female friendly policies such as time off work, family support, day care support and economic incentives to have children. Not foster irrational hatred of other people for having been born different from the present "norm." Cultural biases against women such as occurred in China, where males vastly outnumber females, due to their one child policy and cultural valuation of male heirs, have created a rapidly aging population that threatens the very survive of the Chinese people into the 21 century. India's treatment of women, seen in the all too frequent headlines of gang rape and child molestations, all because they were girls and of lesser value in the mind of their attackers, shows the horrors of third world women. When they escape those shores for a haven of hope, while not perfect, we allow women their choices. Including when and where to have children, how many to have and so on. This is the core of western civilization. The British First movement may live in England, they cannot be said to belong to anything other than to their narrow racist bigotry. Vote as you want for Briexit. But vote with a clear head not clouded in racist fears and bad demographics.

Voter fraud

May 2, 2011, St. Lambert, Quebec, Canada. Election Day.

Voter fraud? Third World Elections Canada Style?

The polls should have opened at 930 am. They did not. There were not enough tables and chairs to set up. So the people were made to wait for 30 minutes. Was no one informed that there would be an election today? Perhaps they forgot to mention it, "oh by the way we might have people who wanted to vote." Mayhap they simply did not have time; after all it was only 40 days ago that the writ was dropped? Was it voter fraud? Which is defined as the deliberate efforts on a person or persons unknown to deprive people of their democratic right to vote? Do not laugh, the riding next door was decided by less than 100 votes the last time. So could 100 people have voted in that 30 minutes of missing time? St. Lambert is a village outside of Montreal where there is a lot of old people, would they have stayed for those 30 minutes? Could they have stood for those 30 minutes? What if it had rained as forecasted? Well, I think we will never know. Will those 30 minutes be returned to the voters of St. Lambert? Of course not, they have to close on time. Schedules to keep, votes to be counted and a third period in the hockey game to watch no doubt.

As far as I know, no one was hurt, shot or killed but this delay. The police were not called out to restore order. The army was not deployed to prevent voters voting. The news is filled with such type of event as other people and other places fight for their rights to vote. Yet in cynical Canada, where we have trouble getting people to care that there is an election going on, Elections Canada also forgot to care as well. Was it voter fraud? Was it an attempt to deprive Canadians citizens of their right to vote? I don't know. But I do this, we could have done better, we should have done better, we must do better.

So where is the urgency? After all it was most probable just a clerical error, a typo or a truck with a flat tire. Yet if one single voter was turned off by the delay and left not to return then their rights have been taken from them. As surely as if someone with a gun had turned them away using force. So I write this letter as the song says to, "Stand on guard for thee;" to protect democracy; to protect my right as a citizen and as a voter. To stand up for those same rights and say to all who will listen, my vote counts. My right to vote will not be infringed upon and when you do so, there is a price to pay, a penalty to be extracted. Even if this is merely a complaint to embarrass Elections Canada, someone has noticed there mistake and someone cares enough to make it an issue.

Signed

A Citizen

A Voter

Someone who cares about democracy.

A Specter is Haunting Montreal

Dateline Montreal

Maple Spring

Students are in the street protest fee increases.

A specter is haunting Montreal the specter of ... of what indeed? It is clear to the citizens of Quebec that a criminal terroristic organization has arrived to impose its outrageous demands in the face of legitimate legislative law. Those reporters who are not writing in the proscribed correct manner to support the criminal organization in its efforts to thwart legitimate government will be dealt with. One can only assume that this sort of threat implies physical violence. Since the criminal organization tactics has used it in the past, it is no leap to assume there will be greater and greater demands upon the citizens to surrender further and further rights to terrorist hooligans. This criminal organization will negotiate and then when a deal is struck immediately back out showing they have wasted more time and were never there in good faith. Law and order has broken down, as students wishing to return to class have won judicial approval of their acts only to find that more criminals continue to openly defy law and order in full view of police. Thus showing an increased alarming trend towards a state of nature on the streets of Quebec; which is similar to the Lord of the Fly, a book also about school age children, where legitimate authority has broken down.

Sadly, I speak of the student so called protesters who should in future merely be referred to as a criminal terroristic organization so as not to be confused with real, legitimate law obeying students. Some fringe elements of the student body as a whole are frustrated in that their voice is not heard. However, take two competing demonstrations. The first demonstration with 500 members of an association of retired people; the Premier himself Jean Charest comes out, offers them coffee and sits and talks for half an hour and the people go home, The premier immediately calls a special session of the legislature to address their concerns and alter legislations. The second is a student protest of 500 000 students. No one offers then coffee and no one listens or cares. The difference? Those 500 retirees represent a voting bloc that votes north of 90% and they are all grandmothers and grandfathers who will express their concerns at Sunday supper to the family. The student forgot there was an election, might have mentioned something important but they drank too much and oh look Stephen Colbert is on and what were we talking about.

In this latest round of student unrest, one student was heard to utter on local TV that this is just like Libya. Showing just what a lousy education he was getting and how badly misinformed, he was in his actions. This is a battle over an increase in taxation. No more and no less. However, the government cannot afford to lose. And it cannot back down or the next time it increases taxes on any one area the province will be held hostage by the likes of a few. The government must however address this issue and do so to break the will of the striking terrorist. To do so the government must crack down: 1) all protestors to be charged not as protesters but as gang members of a criminal terroristic organization. 2) Outlaw any and all groups that support said criminal terrorist organization including student unions. 3) Demand that all Student unions denounce any all forms of violence and call off this illegal strike immediately. 4) Any student group that does not, should face fines of 1000$ per person, 100 000$ per executive, and 1 million for the group's umbrella union. These are similar fines imposed on striking teachers and nurses so why not on students? 5) The school year ends on June 15 or around there for CEGEP Professors. All summer schools or elongation of the term to make up for lost time; basically costing the tax payers more money we have already paid for once, that was rejected in favor of this strike should be denied. Grades are due in and should be based on whatever grades teachers have in their hand, based on work already handed in. If that fails a large number of students then they should be forced to reapply in 2 years as is the normal procedure for failed students.

Long after, students are routinely paying the still lowest tuition fee in Canada, and everyone else has forgot their acts of terrorism, these people should be regretting their crimes against society while still in jail. Where there will be no beer bashes, and there are no special privileges. This is not medieval Paris, and the students have no benefit of clergy to escape civil law. It is time the government step up and do their job of restoring civil order, democracy and start arresting the terrorists.

Mr. Prime minister

Dear Mr Prime Minister

I work for Canada post. Sort of. See, I just got promoted to part time but, well you can read below all about that "but."

See I started as Christmas helper. But that offered me no real job, just some money to help out at Christmas. Then 5 months later, they offered me a real job, or so I thought, but it was not really a job. It was a position as a temporary employee. Meaning, I got little to no work for long periods of time, only called in as needed. They say in HR to keep your second job, even as the supervisors say "No" you should only work at Canada Post. In fact, many of the people hired when I was, quit to find other jobs that paid them a regular salary or 40 hours of paid work. As I got up the ladder in seniority, three long years to climb it, I was finally appointed, just last month, to a part time position. Can you imagine any job that takes three years to get just to part time? Not yet full time, just part time. To get a full time job, they tell me could take another two years. And what a lofty position this part time job is, I only get 20 hours a week which works out to a little less that 300$ per week. But the co0rperation says even that is too much.

I went to pay my bills today. Sadly, had to cut corners, as I did not make enough money last pay to afford everything I had to pay this time. Can you imagine that? A civil servant, living high off the fatted cow, did not making enough money? I make 300$ or less net per week. My parents were middle class. Now, better educated then they were, I have 5 university degrees, including 2 Master of Arts and with a "good" job the Government of Canada, I have fallen, along with the rest of Canada from such middling aspirations. The middle class no longer exists. Good thing I am used to living off my credit cards because that is how I afford to make ends meet. Those bank card are where the profits from my interest goes to private banks, not the general good or the general public as postal banking might help us all out with. But I guess since the Deepak Chopra is the President and CEO of Canada Post, this idea won't happen. After all, the private sector banking might not like it if there was a bank in rural communities that did not start with the phrase "Pay Day Loans". Or if people who want to work, actually earned enough to pay off their bills and get out of debt and could afford to think of themselves as middle class. I guess that sort of middle class Canadian dream died on the order paper in Harper's government agenda to Americanise Canada to more business friendly country. Tory times are hard times. Don't worry, they tell me that 23% interest is a fair rate for long term credit card debt.

I checked out my projected retirement income using a projection calculator offered by Canada Post. I cheated on what I filled the form in with. I imputed the amount of a full time employee, as if I were suddenly promoted to full time, as if... (Remember they say another 2 or more years for that.) What I would earn when I retired at the age of 71 after 25 years of service? Almost what I am earning now per week, only per month. They tell me that Canada Post has to cut my luxurious pension even more with this round of contract negotiations. This Cadillac of pension plans is too rich to sustain itself. I would work more and longer than age 71 but they say I cannot. I have to take my pension at 71. Now like Peter Mackay, former Tory Defense Minister, he will get 150 000$ per year starting from age 55 and on for the rest of his life. It would take me 500 months or near 42 years to earn that much money he will earn per year. Good thing he gets that all free from the Canadian Tax Payers. I guess there are two classes of people. Former Tories and their rich friends and the working poor who's pension are just too luxurious to afford any longer.

Tory times are hard times, unless you are part of the elect of Tory inner circles.

What would I know about paying taxes, since I don't earn really enough to pay taxes? You would think working for the federal government; I would earn a decent living, perhaps to dream of being middle class? But since Tory times are hard times, there is no more decent living to be had in Canada, unless you get a bonus. How much does Canada Post pay out in bonuses? I know I am surely not getting any. They only go to rich. Being working poor, you would think after 3 years I would be somewhat better off. But it's so hard to make any money with so few hours! The corporation does not want to offer too many full time jobs. After all, then people might earn a living. My salary won't go up either. Wages are too high as it. They have a deficit. Except they earned a profit last year. But none the less wages are too high! They keep cutting jobs, no more full time position to be had, only part time and they want to cut those as well. Part time to be flexible, so flexible they don't even care about the people doing those jobs. That is their problem, not Canada Post's problem. In fact, at Canada Post, they want to cut my old wages as a temporary employee to one salary for the length of the contract, to make the poor people who take those jobs even more hard pressed. They also want to reduce vacation from three weeks to two weeks, what would I know about taking a vacation? As a temp, I never took vacation, if I did not work, I did not get paid. That would be where the work part of working poor comes in. But with the contract being negotiated, (sorry Canada Post is not interested in negotiating, they are just waiting to illegally lock us out again then get punitive back to work legislation) Canada Post wants to remove all that and more including my paid lunch. Well, the paid lunch that a full timer gets. I don't get one being part time. I bring in a muffin. I make it from home. I cannot afford to eat out much. Not like the executive dinning that President

Chopra and the 23 executive Vice Presidents get. This is sad, because my local restaurants are all struggling with the same problem, too many working poor, not enough people spending money on take out or dinning. No one can afford to eat out any more. Tory times are hard times.

I suppose I should smile but as a temporary employee I don't qualify for benefits like dental. So I have not seen my dentist in years. Cause any sort of benefit is too good for us. In fact, nothing is too good for us and that is exactly what we get... Nothing. Tory times and all that...

I hear that Canada Post made a profit the last few years. Which is strange because it was not too long ago that a think tank, (ask President Chopra what the name is, since he is a member, I am sure long since forgotten by everyone else) said Canada Post would be losing a billion dollars a year by now. They earned a profit every year since that report came out. With friends like that, publishing a such tripe bias hit piece to start the ball rolling for back to work legislation with the last Tory government, just like they are trying to do now. Just like they did last time, make a series of impossible demand that force a strike call. When the workers act collectively, the corporation illegally locks them out so said the arbiter in our collective grievance. Then the Tory government passes an illegal back to work law in Parliament (Again as an Ontario Judge has said no less in June of this year) that takes away 1% of wages that the corporation had already agreed to in negotiations just for Tory spite. How nasty is that? The corporation offers an increase that the Tories legislate away from the workers... I wonder if they took away anyone's bonus like that. Or retirement plan? It took the union many years of fighting this before a judge ruled that law unconstitutional. And rightly so! But since we are not part of the elite, the rich or in bed with the Tories, those of us who are working poor, that would be the majority of Canadians, we just don't count as being important enough to get a fair deal.

See Prime Minister; they are trying to do the same thing now. Force the workers to strike. Lock them out then run to you for back to work legislation. That is unfair. And worse, they tried it before and lost in the courts. How many more times will they use the same play book? When will they start to fairly negotiate a fair deal with the worker that actually improves the lives of so many Canadians?

As you know, North Carolina passed a horrible bill to limit the accessibility to toilets for transgender people. What did we do in Canada? Your government enshrined the rights of transgendered people into our human rights legislation. In Quebec, with the full approval of the opposition parties, yes more than one opposition party all agreed to allow transgender people the right to change their school name and sex in order to allow them a better chance at assimilation in high school. Can you see the difference between Donald Trump's America and Canada? Where would you put Canada Post and their present administration on that scale? Are they going to do the right thing? The fair thing? The Canadian way? Or will they resort to crushing the working poor with illegal lock out and unconstitutional back to work legislation in Parliament.

Tory times are hard times. You are a liberal. Will you follow the old model of nasty hate? Or is it 2016, and times they are a changing?

In 1949, you father, Pierre Elliott Trudeau, covered the strike by mine workers at Thetford Mines. Where Quebec Premier Maurice Duplessis sided with the rich mine owners, to send in his goon squads to break the union. Your father stood with the worker and went on to be a force of good for the people Canada, all the people of Canada, not just the wealthy elites but for the working poor. So I ask you Prime Minister, when we strike at Canada Post, will you come to do a shift on the picket line? They last 4 hours, twice a week. We get paid 200$ per week. Where will you stand? With whom will you walk with?

Canada Post

I have known about the consultation for the future of Canada Post for a while now. I felt; "Why should I speak, I had nothing to say, the union had said it all: Return to home to home delivery, postal expansion into more areas of delivery like groceries and the much hyped postal banking." I had nothing to add to that. That is, until now. So the question being, what do you foresee as the future of Canada Post? I reply with my own question; will there even be a future for Canada Post?

To wit, let us exam this issue. The Minister, Judy Foote has asked Canada Post to explore service expansion. The union is more than willing to do that including pushing for the return of postal banking, and yet the corporation does nothing. Thus leaving what could be a large new area for the future and future business left wanting. So I ask why?

The union want to negotiate a new contract. The government wants this matter settled as well! Yet the corporation refuses to come to the negotiation table. Giving one and only one offer then saying they are done. This is not negotiating under anyone definition. "Take it or leave it;" is not an opening gambit for a resolution. The result is for customer business to lose confidence in the corporation, seek other providers and general hurt the business all around by their own action or inaction on senior management. Again I must ask why?

Why would a business deny expansion when it can easily do so.?

Why would it sabotage its already existing business?

Why would it alienate a work force that is nothing but professional?

Why indeed?

When the Conservative Government took over under Brian Mulroney, they expect that the public servants, so long working for the previous liberal governments would hesitate to bring in conservative legislation or fulfill their goals. So to make sure their policies were respected, they created a number of positions staffed by hand pick conservatives to watch over the process and make sure the government will was respected. In the end, it was found they were not needed. The public servants of Canada respected the will of the people and followed through on the government will. Yet the present day, clear government will, to expand postal services and settle this contract, is not being respected? I again ask why? By what right or obligation would public servants disobey in spirit if not in action their role to follow government directives? What outside Ideology or influence is so powerful that it would call them to their higher authority then their oath of office? And that is where it hit me.

The Neo Conservatives in the USA have their own right wing. The right wing has a right wing making it even more right wing than normal. They call themselves the Tea Party. Their philosophy is that all government is bad, and anything that is good for business interests is good. No matter if it hurts the interest of the working class.

If we put this all together we can begin to see a pattern.

Expanding the government is verboten; opening up postal banking would hurt private banks, and pay day loans, also Forbidden. Having a happy productive work force is not necessary. In fact, the more unhappy, the more likely people are to quit and thus one less person on the government workforce, making government that much smaller. In sum, Canada Post is acting as if under the control of a group of right wing ideologies with Tea Party sympathies, if not outright allegiances. Their goal is to ruin Canada Post for future generation by destroying it from the inside at every step.

The solution, radical for North America perhaps, but also tried and true for Europe is a new direction must be called for and this includes new blood in the executive suit. Many European countries have created corporation laws where the union is not the enemy but on the board itself. Called Codetermination, it is in part the law in such countries as Germany, Austria and Switzerland. By including the workers and their representatives, there is less strife and more harmony. Both sides work together to make the company the best it can be.

If there is to be a future for Canada Post, it needs to enter the 21 century with a new governing body to oversee the place, made up with progressive thinkers and including the union in the same way they do it in Europe. This body would be in charge of oversight on the day to day running of Canada Post. And most importantly, it would be able to explore a growing future for change that includes all stakeholders. Rather than the stagnant, Tea Party, out for destruction, unwilling to change body we have now in upper management. If there is to be a future of Canada post, we need to secure it now, with the right sort of people inside the institution able to foster change but also willing to be a part of change as well.

justin.trudeau@parl.gc.ca

judy.foote@parl.gc.ca

Alexandra.Mendes@parl.gc.ca

MaryAnn.Mihychuk@parl.gc.ca

feedback@cupw-sttp.org

Justine Trudeau and new legislation

An open Letter to Prime Minister Justin Trudeau

Congrats on the win, now it is time to get to work. Bring forth a legislative agenda to rock Canada with progressive legislation that helps clear the way from the destruction left by Stephen Harper's government.

1) Legalise Marijuana. You ran on this, time to deliver. But, least this become a freak show, free for all, it must have limits. I think that we need to commercialise it and tax it. The best way to do so is treat it as if it was a new round of cigarettes. Simple as that! Collect tax revenue from it as well.

2) Call off your tired old morals or something like that. The courts ruled the old prostitution laws where unconditional. So the Harper government brought in even worse laws. Get rid of them all. Again legalise it, make it a legitimate business and then, you got it, tax it. Require a license, that needs a medical exam, and a check or proof the person is over 18, and we cut out organized crime, the trafficking of women to fill this niche and under age prostitution. Best of all, we collect GST on the whole exchange.

3) Pass private member bill C-204, or whatever it will be called, allowing for gender identity and gender expression added to the Canadian Human Rights Act and the Criminal Code. A Canadian is a Canadian is a Canadian. Let's add one of the most vulnerable groups to becoming full citizens.

People say this is all too simplistic. We need to study the ramifications of this all before we go forward. Really? *"Insanity: doing the same thing over and over again and expecting different results." Albert Einstein.* Let's try something new. In one draft we have added two new sources of sin tax to Revenue Canada's collection plate, decriminalized many acts that people were going to do regardless of what the law says, and last we embrace a sub group of Canadians who have been sorely abused by our neglect.

But wait, you think that is radical? I have one more thing to say. If the above is radical, then the next piece of advice is revolutionary. Surely, it will burn down Main Street in its wake. But... the tax revenue it will generate will be enormous. Take the follow, you go to the store and buy yourself some chips and a coke. You pay the lady at the counter the price for both and she charges you provincial sales tax and Good and Services Tax from the federal government. In Quebec, this amounts to some 15.5% which is a large bit out of your wallet. I will only ask that we collect the same amount of taxes that corporations are charging! I suggest that we tax all stock trades at 1.5% of purchase price. This is the same amount that you will get charged by the trading company or trader that you deal with. The difference is this. Whereas GST hits all Canadians as a regressive tax, this tax only affects the very wealthy and the rich. The TSX could generate tax revenue nearing 3 million dollars per day, perhaps as much as a billion dollars per year or more. Best of all, this sort of tax effects only the wealthiest of people and spares the middle class from its reach. Same deal for my last suggestion. Presently, there is no inheritance tax for wealthy Canadians. So for those with estates worth over 100 million dollars, we should charge them 1%. The counter is that this money was already taxed once and would now be taxed a second time. While this is true, the money belongs to a dead person who seemingly no longer has any use for it. But seriously, the money was made by the help of Canadian society to raise it, safe guard it and now can be used again to help Canadians. The only people who would complain are those who inherit it. They are merely not getting as much as they would have and 1% less is hardly noticeable for the estate. But it will help out the deficit and other social needs of Canadians.

So in short, here is a legislative agenda bordering on revolutionary. Best of all, it amounts to untapped sources of revenue that government can use to pay from infrastructure, education and health care. These bills that are due today and need funding at an ever increasing amount will need to be paid from somewhere. New sources for revenue must be found. And the middle class cannot be where the money comes from. They already pay their share. Take a small bit from the rich or charging people tax on new forms of legal entertainment are a great way to help out the public purse.

Ruth Ellen

How does one defend the Prime Minister after he brutally attacked Ruth Ellen Brosseau? A sharp, hard, cruel elbow to the chest, followed up by forcing her to relive the moment over and over again as he constantly referred to it in his frequent apologises. Such pathos, such drama, such melodrama! Or rather what a load of ... The problem with this narrative is this; the NDP members were blocking the conservative whip. Justine Trudeau came over to escort the whip to the speaker's chair, rescuing him from a mob of NDP obstructionists. Wherein the jostling; Ruth Ellen Brosseau was struck in the chest. Lightly, (An NDP member pushed the whip, who in turn bounced off Trudeau, which then pushed Trudeau's elbow that hit Brosseau) but she immediately took the dive for all the screen actor credits she could get, all the while acting as if she had been assaulted and injured. Thomas Mulcair the disgraced NDP leader immediately took up the outrage as if this had been a deliberate, vicious assault upon her being. As if this was the greatest crime of the century, as if... And here in lies the whole point. What Mulcair and Brosseau fail to grasp is this; Canadians are not stupid. We can see the video, we can see the faux outrage and we can see the disingenuous hyperbole from the NDP on this issue. There is a reason why they, the NDP voted Mulcair out of his job as head of the party; this very disingenuous behavior on his part. Contrast that with his predecessor, Jack Layton. Like him or hate him, he was a genuine person in the way he talked, acted and behaved. Jack was the real deal, not some ready to scream outrage at any issue, any issue at all, no matter how small they may be as Mulcair clearly is ready to do, showing that this type of "woe's me" crying is all the voters could see from him. Thus, they punished the NDP in the last election by voting for the Liberals and remove most of the NDP Party's historic gains under Jack Layton to another genuine person, Justine Trudeau. This is what drives this faux outrage by the former head of the NDP. The simple fact that Canadians like Justine Trudeau. They like what they see and what they have seen so far. The poll numbers don't   lie   either. (http://www.cbc.ca/news/politics/grenier-quarterly-polls-mar2016-1.3469716) If an election was held now, he might get a super majority on top of the majority he already had. So Thomas, scream all you want. It has worked out so well for you this far. Ruth, you need to watch more soccer to see how the professions fake a dive. You are not very good at it.

SOS Same Old Stuff

The Liberal nomination in the riding of Saint-Laurent, was supposed to be for Yolanda James, the star candidate, former MNA and cabinet minister in the provincial government. She was all but appointed to run for that riding, considered to be one of safest in Canada for Liberals. The Liberal organization practically decreed that James should get it, heavily lobbying people to vote for her. In fact, they turned down long serving St-Laurent borough mayor Alan DeSousa who was blocked for reasons unknown by the party from also running. Conspiracy theorists claiming that he was blocked in order to let James take the seat. It was not long before we heard the painfully repetitive cry of "Shame" without any hint of the schadenfreude underlying the pointed finger. All the while their own hypocrisy is left to slide away. The liberals say they have changed but look the pundits cry, they have not changed at all. Same old back room dealing and same old roughshod over the local people to impose their big bad will on them. Except? For people who are in the news business should they not read the actual facts? Alan DeSousa was blocked, no reason given. How about he was one of the long term mayors that worked around all the corruption in Montreal and did nothing about it? How about the party was trying to distance itself from that same old legacy of being surrounded by the "Sponsorship Scandal" which it could not if even a hint or smell of corruption came with DeSousa? Or could it be they just don't want to take on his baggage so they let him down gently with a polite but firm, "No thanks." As for the process; let democracy be the judge is the new policy. Last time I checked, free speech was part of that so called Democracy. So the party saying, "James is a great person who will do you proud if you select her as your representative for your riding;" is very much a long way from parachuting her into the riding without holding a vote. James showing her class when she tweeted her congratulations to the winner. The very same person elected by the riding itself. Same old what? Same old democracy speaking, perhaps? There is shame to be had here but it is merely the shadow of talking heads mired in a past best left behind by all concerned. Oh and the lady who won? Emmanuella Lambropoulos, a 26-year-old high school teacher who now has a new career and considering how safe her seat is, she may be in politics for a very long while. Good for her. She won by going door to door and rallying the people to her side. She also just happens to live in her riding that she will represent. Who would have thought when the Liberal party said things have changed that they would let some unknown political novice be elected into one of their fortresses. Unheard of. Indeed, even unthinkable. And this act of direct democracy in action is being called shameful? Same old Liberals? Hip hip hooray! Let's have more of this "Old Song and Dance" again. And let the people decide who they want to represent them. Oh wait, the Liberals already have in this riding. More power to them all! People power.

Feudalism

When dealing with the American election, people are struggling to define the so call economic model that presently exists within the USA. They have called it with such vague descriptors as corporate capitalism, or crony capitalism, but they have thus far failed to grasp the exact nature of this system. They keep reaching for new explanations, when a perfectly good one lies hidden in plain sight, but not from the present, it comes from the past. What other economic system exists where 1% holds 99% of the wealth? Where the religious leaders tell people that this is the divine plan and they should simple hope for better in the afterlife. Where the class one is born to, marks the person for life. This system was called Feudalism. It very much has returned to the land of the free, home of the brave called these United States.

The American case has some specific modern twists. The first leg of this tripod comes from Russian refuge Ayn Rand, for whom we refer to in philosophy as among the groups of irrationals. She has an extensive body of work where she posits that greed is the only good. So long as I am looking out for number one, the rest will follow. The second leg of our tripod is the Protestant system of "Election", (To be among those elected by Christ.) Not be confused with anything to do with voting. By this we call to mind, that God has ordained people to be the elect, into his grace. Those who have an automatic ticket into heaven, no matter what they do on Earth, they have been elected or chosen to everlasting life. So no matter how much harm, misery or suffering they cause, they have their place reserved for them in the paradise to come. This takes a load off the mind from worrying about what is to come. This also applies to corporations and their fiduciary responsibility to maximise profit no matter the social consequences. So long as they follow the mandates of cooperate election, to maximise profits, they can do no wrong. Lead by executives who also lack any sense of morality, for they are "Elect" of God, the combination is a single minded focus that destroys as many lives as needed to maximise the bottom line for the company and share holders. The last pillar comes from the social aspect of race, specifically that the so called "White Race" which in this doctrine is seen as superior to the again, so called "Black and / or Brown Races." Selfish greed, elect by God and superior to all people, whatever could go wrong with such a combination? All three aspects tend to be different iterations of the same sort policy goals that the so called capitalistic market place in the USA endorses. I got mine and to hell with you. In this case, literally, to hell with you.

Breaking each aspect down further, we begin with the notion of greed. In Adam Smith ideal economy there is the trickledown theory. The rich can only consume so much wealth and thus in their exuberance, they allow plenty to pass down to enrich the lower classes. Sadly, this is based on the notion that goods and services expire, they break or wear out or in the case of food, spoils. When this happens there is a constant need for replacement so that the lower class that produces the goods and services consumed by the upper class, are then enriched in the making or selling such goods to those in the upper class. This is not the case of modern economy where ideas mean more. They have no time limit or expiration date. By this we call to mind stocks, bonds and other assets that are not tangible, immoveable things. A joint stock company may own immovable's, like manufacturing plants, buildings, furniture. But the stocks in that corporation are nothing but pieces of paper, on in this computer age, dots on the screen. This is a mental construct of ownership of any given company. The owner of stock need not replace or repair it, as stock will not wear out, or break down. The ownership is constant and so too is the income from profits. They simple accept the wealth and benefits from ownership including unlimited future earnings that are taxed lower than income, as this wealth is seen as privileged wealth that creates jobs. If only this was still the case today. Thus the wealthy are able to amass greater and greater control in their hands while not having to spend any of that capital to maintain their so called "Property". Whereas a rich person might spend some or very little of their money, they literally are taking the wealth and freezing it away from the economy as they purchase more and more stocks and bonds. A poor person, needing all their money to pay bills and survive, commonly seen as living paycheque to paycheque, dispense all the case they have and are often forced to borrow more money be it on credit from credit cards or worse Payday Loan shops. This in turn creates record profits for both industries that are in this vicious loop, and ultimately returned to rich people. A rich person given a dollar would ignore it as they have many more. A poor person would spend that money as they have none of their own.

Therefore, in order to spur the economy, create new jobs, and grow the country itself, the tax burden must be returned to the wealthy, who simply are not using their wealth, in order to transfer the tax burden from the lower and middle class who will in turn spend this money adding to the economy. What blocks this is the greed of the rich who wish to hold on to what they own. Note that I did not call this selfish, as it might be in some cases, but it might not be as well. We all hate paying taxes. We all hate unfairness and we all hate to be singled out. But when the top 1% of 1% of the American people earn as much as the bottom 20%, it is not a time for increasing tax breaks for the rich or reducing their income tax. When corporations pay a tax rate lower than a poor person existing at the poverty line, there is something wrong with this picture. Sadly, the American dream is purchased and sold to those same rich people. There is no will to assist the poor or the middle class. There is however, a lot of incentive to help the rich donor class, as they will give money to future elections, jobs, and other perks to impress people into enacting legislation that will benefit themselves and only themselves. Because they are the elites. The poor are those cursed by God, coloured people or simple those who are too weak to be selfish in their own right.

Where there is no justice, there can be no peace. This lesson was learned in Europe in the 19th century as the lower class would rise up in rebellion and try to over throw the existing order, and execute the wealthy oppressors. In time, it became clear to the wealthy they might be elected by God, but they might want to live to a ripe old age to not rush to meet their maker, rather than be left swinging on the apple tree in their yard. At some point, the overwhelming majority of people who make up the lower and middle class will turn to violence and they will enact their vengeance. Wake up before it is too late. Make social justice your rallying cry! Not self enrichment, lacking empathy to all who are not as lucky as you. Stocks are made of paper. They burn just as well as factories do, as well as rich people hanging from their gallows. The only question left before us is this, how will America solve its problems? By accord, or by the sword? Time will answer this.

No Corporate tax

Just say no to corporate taxes!

I know that sounds just so right wing. Donald Trump anyone? How about if was in fact left wing and progressive? When you have a tax that hits everyone equally, it is considered regressive. A progressive tax is one that increases as your ability to pay increase. So rich people pay more and poor people pay less. Corporate tax on profit is paid for by the buyer equally. Since a corporation has no independent way to raise money except from their clients, those clients are in effect paying for their taxes the corporation will pay on profits. If remove that tax, then in an ideal world the price of goods should drop. It most likely won't as corporations would instead merely increase the amount of profit they take home. And I think that is also an equally good idea. Taxes that corporation pay are usually in the none existent, they find loopholes or tax avoidance schemes to fraud or outright bribery of government officials in order to avoid paying any sort of taxes to begin with. So let's get rid of this sham anyways.

With the extra cash, they might create more jobs. Ok let's pause while we laugh with cynical realism at that so often boasted claim that turns out to be a fictional use of the language bordering on outright lies. They can re-invest those profits into research and development. Which I will assert is a good thing. Since they won't have to fake R&D to avoid paying taxes, the result may be some real progress and real developments that will provide additional resources for the company to make even more money and hence real job growth potential. The other two ways are buying back stock, or providing it to shareholders as dividends or paying executives. I see both as ways to tax that money back properly. First, stock; which are on average held for a grand total time of 23 second before being sold off. This churning makes some people money using computers to buy and sell. The marginal gains on fractions of pennies over millions of shares can yield small but significant profits. If all sells are taxed at a small rate of 2% for the federal government and 1% to the province, real tax revenue would be gains. Simple enough to see, all those profits made on Wall Street and Bay Street is from a surcharge of 1.5% on every sale. They make lots of money, so too should the government collect. Also, since most poor people don't buy significant amounts of shares, the purchase will not adversely affect the middle class or the poor. The cash dividend tax rate is paid for at the rate of 33% but subject to modifications from other tax breaks. Since there is no longer a corporate tax, all dividends are to be taxed at 50% at source and not subject to refund. In other words, you money is gone when you get the cash.

This leaves me with two additional points. CEO's make an unholy amount of money, very little in the form of cash but the vast majority in stock in their pay package. They get billions in stock. This practise has to stop. All shares are to be granted in the form of cash and taxed at the 50% rate. As well, it will be part of the financial fillings, in case it is not, that all such salaries are quoted in cash so stock holders, even unsophisticated investors can see just how much the CEO is taking from their bottom line.

Lastly, without the need to lower tax rates, corporations might be tempted to stop sponsoring charities and sporting events. After all, they don't get the tax break they used to. Fortunately, I rather doubt they do give away money in an effort to be good corporate citizens. They do it from the advertisement and the tax breaks. I know so young and yet so cynical. They will still sponsor those charities, perhaps not as much, but they still will continue to give. Why? Because it is a form of free advertising and being seen as a bad corporate citizen or worse greedy would harm their bottom line where they make profits from to begin with.

I think this will clean up the tax act, and greatly increase tax revenue. By fairly taxing the people making the money, not the corporations who are just too good at hiding it from the taxman, we get our, society as a whole, fair share of taxes from the rich. This would make the tax progressive, and fair as only the very rich would be paying such taxes on traded stock and dividends.

3. Fairness

Black Lives Matter

In order to understand the trouble that vexes the United States with recent events, it is important to understand elements of their socio-economic class and racial structure: White Privilege and Black lives.

It is very hard to explain what white privilege is to a white person. Just as it is hard to explain to a male what male privilege is from a female perspective. For in both cases, they say what privilege? They do see the problem walking anywhere, at anytime, wearing anything they want. Whites simply do not interact with police, so what privilege is that? Never seeing that based on being white the police will not stop them for any reason other than the colour or lack of colour in their skin. However for someone black, they do interact in absurd amounts with police compared to the whites. Diamond Reynolds calmly recorded her boyfriend dying in the seat next to her after he was brutally shot by one nervous cop. Being that she, as a black female, was so often stopped by police for no reason, getting upset would not change anything, let alone prevent anything from happening. Male privilege means they don't have to be as weary of the next corner because if preyed upon it would be for their wallet not what was under their clothing. So they too can calmly walk through a storm that would leave other who are not used to such behavior completely affected with fear and dread.

The concept of privilege is one that can only be seen from the perspective of one who does not have it. Just as entitlement is alien to whoever is so privileged and has the rights to be entitled. From the pauper view however, it is very different. They can see up, the privileged must be challenged to see down. There is a national best seller, but clearly 50 or more years old called "Black Like me" by John Howard Griffin (published 1961) where a white man walks in the shoes of being black in the south. Changes his race to cross the colour barrier and see what life is like on the other side of the coin. This book tells the tales from his journey. You can see the way he is treated what privilege is. Or in a more humorist vein Eddie Murphy does a skit on Saturday Night Live about being white; where he dons white makeup to look like a white person. While very funny, it is also very telling too. Clever humour does indeed transcend beyond me laughs into a deep social commentary.

As a white male, I am never suspected of being a criminal just because I am white

As a male I am never looked at as "Asking for it," no matter what I am wearing.

It is only when I look at the reality of people of colour or of women do I see the privilege of my existence.

It is only when other people begin to look at the world from the eyes of the "other" that they see the charmed existence we who have the privilege have compared to others.

Three dead cops in Baton Rouge and three injured... by a gunman, details are unclear at this time, but I suspect it will soon be linked to black lives matters as well. For all crime against police comes from Black Lives Matter. And if that makes no sense to you, so what? Anything to discredit that movement will be found and used against them. For nothing is more dangerous than a good idea. Only the privileged need not be bothers to look or to see that. Martin Luther King Jr was subject to black mail over illegal tapes; such as being ordered to commit suicide and other horrible things. And his crime was? Leading a movement to bring equality to all people.

"We must learn to live together as brothers or perish together as fools."

Martin Luther King Jr

As much as the SC shooter, wrapped in the Southern battle flag murdering people in a black church, Dallas and Baton Rouge were both acts of mad men. But armed with military weapons and free access to purchase as many as they can carry or could carry... This is the inevitable result. Where blacks armed themselves and confronted police in the streets of California, Ronald Reagan, as governor signed some of the harshest carry laws in the USA with the full support of the NRA. Carrying guns is a right only to the privilege and being black with a gun is seemingly an executable offense in Minnesota or it was for Philando Castile.

The cause is always the same, injustice, videotaped injustice, which is now finally making its appearance on TV and the internet that will force politicians and police to demand better answers. If all cops had cameras, and all the stops where recorded, then the often heard cry of abuse, racial profiling and racism would be there to be seen and view and best of all, reviewed. Accountability would have to kick in. Most cops are good people. The bad apples are the ones they need to be found and removed from office. Let them work in sanitation and be as hateful as they want to be. They give all police, a bad name. In Dallas, while the crowds were running from the violence. The men and women in blue were running towards it. When Shetamia Taylor was shot by the sniper in Dallas, she and her son that she was shielding, were, in turn, shielded by police officers. There to serve and protect, they served her by protecting her and getting her to a hospital in a vehicle shot up by the sniper. She is black, they were white. To then look at this issue as only a black and white thing, is to miss the point. It is not colour but of power that is often reflected in a white on black thing. But similar tales are found in all white communities where the white police pick on lower socio-economical privileged whites. It's not the skin, it's the power.

Sadly, I do suspect that what has started in Dallas and now Baton Rouge will accelerate and continue as more and more cops will be ambushed in the coming days. But without a resolution, or solution in sight this will be just another story soon forgotten as more and more are killed. Cops are focused on their weapons and military tactics to deal with type of event on average of 180 hours of training and practise. Yet any possible solution would be found in de-escalation and non lethal force. How much training would they get in that on average? Only 24 hours. 180 hours to kill, 24 hours to control and de-escalate... Seems we have one clearly visible, low hanging fruit to pick off with ease.

American cops taken to a target range with a simulated battle field exercise; they walk around an obstacle course only with the chances to shot. They are then faced with various pop ups of either criminals and or civilians and have to decide to shot or hold fire. The fastest time win. Scientists using this for controlled experiments where they are secretly measuring the reaction time in the decision to shot or to hold fire. Studies show that they take half as long to decide to shot a black face than a white face. This is not a training issue. This is cultural issue. If your head is filled with the insulting stereotypes that refer to the "other" as dangerous predators (Ask Hilary Clinton about that one...). You approach the "Other" like wild, dangerous animals. Shoot first out of fear to protect yourself. 26% of all shooting victims by police are black. Yet blacks make up only 15% of the population. The only way to break that barrier down is to familiarize white cops with black families and brown and Asian and everything else until they see those "others," are not "others" at all but the same as you are, people not predators. Humans with hopes and dreams who also want to go home at the end of their encounter with police.

The Dallas police chief encouraged disenfranchised black youth to join the police force so they can patrol and protect their own communities. To help build a better tomorrow by showing positive role models in their home communities and create sorely needed bridges from the police to the minorities that allow both sides a better tomorrow.

While I applaud that very idea, there is one problem. Who is the one class of people who cannot become police? Criminals. What is the one thing most black males all have in common? They have been arrested, charged and convicted of a crime in some places greater than 50% of the male population over 18 years of age. So just who amongst those new bridge builders can they, the police, reach out to for this help, when they have already been precluded from their helping? Vicious circle. No black community members to help so the white cops are an alien invasion force that act like lord high sheriff to the lowly villagers who are in turn regularly abused by those with their police power in the mere fact they are in the community but not a part of it. White cops in Ferguson don't live in Ferguson. That's where the blacks live. They moved out long ago to more white areas. But they surely come back to keep the people in line. Just ask Mike Brown how that worked out for him. I was going to use the word citizens instead of villagers but can that even be said when being treated as a second class citizen would be a step or two up?

For better or for worse, there is a problem. Point fingers at one side of the other will not help. Nor can we be expected to demand from people to be less criminal or get themselves to a position of more power, better income less poverty. What we can do is make sure police are giving the best possible training, and that has to include socio economic field work with minority communities, de-escalation training like they do in Europe where the use of police violence is near unheard of and lastly camera both in car and on cops. When citizen journalists do observe the scene of police interaction, they should be welcome and embraced as being there to keep all sides honest. That won't cure the problem until gun control comes in to remove some of the 300 million firearms around the country from the hands of unstable people who suffer mental health problems. But it will be a start, whose time is overdue.

White Privilege

In part, white privilege does not exist for whites.

Male privilege does not exist for males either.

However, if you are black and or female, only then you can see it. The white male cannot.

As a white male, I can drive all over and never get stopped by the police. The man, Philando Castile, had been stopped something like 31 times and hit with 63 traffic charges in the last 14 years. Total number of times I have been stopped? (Knock on wood) Zero. See no privilege for me. I will just assume that I am a drive better than any African American... But the absence of gains (not being stopped) does not in any way show up when each stop takes 30 minutes to an hour of their time. Yet unless I see beyond my lofty position, that is only privileged from an outsider prospective, I cannot see imagine having any advantage. Cops look at the skin color of the driver. "Oh he is white, so he may be a lawyer, or a judge or he maybe someone important." But when they see black, that is all they see. There are reports on this guy's life, that he was a role model for his students, praised as a local hero to get kids off on the right start. He was always there, always working for his student, his colleges and all that, a stand up guy considered a pillar in his community. Even if only half of that is true, he was more than an asset to his community and the communities at large. He was some needed in every community. All that the cops saw was black. In my case, I doubt very much if I would be so praise, coming anywhere near this guy's involvement. But I am white and thus giving a road pass. The absence of evidence is the evidence of absences that is the evidence itself need, in this case of showing white privilege. A NY city cop recorded his bosses giving him advice. (Paraphrased) Why did he only stop 2 black men? He replied that he stopped the same number of people as he was supposed to but he was lower in the "pop" rate; those people who are wanted on warrants, wanted or whatever, to be detained, arrested or put back in jail. People stopped are said to "pop" when their name is entered and they have issues with law enforcement. The cop goes on to explain that he stops everyone equally regardless of race, or color. He stops those he has legal probable cause to stop. The boss goes; (paraphrased) "Stop the blacks. They pop more. They commit the crimes. More pops means more arrests which in turn mean better performance reviews." Of course that means for the rest of the black males who are not going to pop they will be stopped more often. And who cares if that is a violation of their civil liberties? No one cares because they are black... Not like as if they were white... who might be someone... This is the attitude of cops to blacks. In Canada it would be more of cops to aboriginal thing in most of the country and to a lesser extent to minorities in the cities. Same basic perception from aboriginals here as Americans have in their racial problem with African Americans, only it is just a different ethnic minority sub class of society in Canada, with the same role, same function and stereotypical behavior along with the same poor treatment. We, in Quebec, however, have a standard of decency for our police. A level of expected behavior that is enforceable and controlled by a body that does not have to work with police like Crown prosecutors have to on a daily basis. The Police Ethics commission; they don't judge based on race or familiarity or any other such consideration but on facts as they can ascertain and the ideal of behavior expected of a cop and from police. Should be and where they find fault, the cop is publicly humiliated for having failed to live up to the standard expected of being a police officer. Essentially saying they have been judged wanting of their duties and failed to live to their oath of office. The best part is this; you only have to fill out a paper forum to make a complaint. No need for a lawyer or costs upon the complaint. The Police Ethics Commission take's over and investigate your complain. Including a follow up visits or calls, so that if your complaint is deemed insufficient they will call you or visit to ask for more information; i.e. you say a cop stopped you? Well, what cop? When did it happen? Where did it happen? Badge number? Name? Car number? Every detail they can find so that they can investigate your complaint. Best of all? It is run by civilians who do this full time. Not cop on cop but civvies on cop, bureaucrats on cops. They also do not have any conflict of interest as the prosecutors have when they need to have the cooperation of police to get their cases convicted in court. The Ethic commissions are fair, honest and they have the grudging respect of both sides. So in part, because we have such a body, and I fear I have never heard of one anywhere in the United States, our cops are better behaved and more respectful if only cause they have big brother watching over them, peering across the blue wall. I should add we have such stops in Canada and in Quebec, where a number of black men were pulled over for the crime of driving while black. The number of stops was in one case like 3-8 times before this citizen filed a complaint and won a judgement against the officers because they, the police, were in the wrong. If American cops where more focused on crime prevention and deterrence rather than lock'em up in corporate prisons and throw away the key they might be better at their job.

American blacks and minorities vote Democrat. Nixon and the Republican's "South First" strategy was designed to stop blacks from voting, by first criminalizing them, then depriving them of their right to vote. (In Canada the Supreme Court rules that all citizens must be allowed to vote and that the government must allow voting from prisons.)Thus began the war on crime and the war on drugs. Where white American are convicted of powder cocaine use at the same rate as blacks with crack cocaine use, white will get diverted into treatment with no criminal record, whereas blacks will go to jail, losing their right to vote and forever must stigmatise themselves with having to admit to a criminal record. A white male in Stanford, Brock Allen Turner, raped a woman and got 6 month in jail because it will mess up his life. A Latino man, for a similar crime got 3 years. It was the same judge, Aaron Persky.

Ok I could go on and on...

The point is this;

There is no such thing as white privilege so long as you are a white male. That is the bottom line and is absolute fact. If you are black or other minority and or female, you can spot the difference if only in the absence of the same sort of treatment that a white male takes for granted. "What do you mean white males are treated differently?" of course not on they will say. Others see the difference because there is the absence of similar treatment (That blacks are subjected to frequently) does not mean it does not exist. Just they cannot see it. Until they do... things won't change.

In North Miami, a black man with his hands up in surrender, lying on his back, in the street, is shot three times by a SWAT officer who was trying to hit a stationary man who was a sitting target. There are so many thing wrong here. 1) Three shots is not an accident discharge. 2) SWAT are trained to shot, he hit what he was aiming for. 3) Why was he shooting in the first place? The man was telling the police he was a mental health professional with a client in distress. No gun was involved. No one was in any danger until the police showed up. At the republican Convention, a sheriff, David A. Clarke Jr. of Milwaukee County,

Wisconsin, boldly asserted that Blue Lives Matter. Well that is true. All lives matter. So why did this man's life not matter? The main point here for black lives matter is this, One is too many, period. So instead of bemoaning the existence of Black Lives Matter, instead of trying to shift blame on to blacks, black culture or anyone else, assume and accept that the blame rest squarely on the shoulders of law enforcement. And then do something about. The point is not merely to enumerate the problem. The point of leadership is to find lasting, effective solutions to these problems. And when you put a challenge to the leadership, you have to put forward your own solutions. That is a responsibility under taken when one criticise the police, the question is well what "your" answer is. Well here is mine.

Every cop needs a body camera. Ever squad car does too. Police need Federal guidelines and standards that ensure police receive de-escalation training and effective familiarization with minority communities and the mentally handicapped or special needs. Finally, all states need a police Ethics commission run independently of police, having no other association with the police and their behavior or with the courts, other than to adjudicate the actions of police against their own guidelines. With a budget that allows them to investigate and either to exonerate or convict police of wrong doing, imposing penalties of fines, suspensions and termination of employment. That is where we will see that there is no need for protest movements. Efforts to bring cops to heel will be first the recordings, then what is in the cameras in the cars. Then they review of federal Guidelines by an impartial body that will run, yes this was justified or it was not. Period. Final word. Until then we can expect escalation and more violence on the part of protesters who are clearly not getting their message heard and this will continue to inevitable lead to more death and more shooting as police feel even more embattled and even more isolated from the communities they patrol.

_____

Black Lives Matters by the numbers

White people make up 62% of the US population. Black people only account for 13% of the same population, or nearly 5 white persons per every single black person in society. Of all the people shot and killed by police, White people are shot by police in 49% of incidents. A 13% difference then the expected result. White should be shot more, if they were being shot was in proportion to their numbers in the makeup of the population. Black's are shot and killed by police 24% of the time, an 11% difference from their percentage of the population if they were in proportion. In fact, black people are almost shot twice as much as their population numbers would indicate. This is a significant difference. Whites are killed by police less than their proportion of the population would indicate and blacks are overly targeted by police.

13% of all black people who are shot and killed by police are unarmed. Compared that to only 7% of whites being unarmed when shot by police. Again twice as many black are killed while unarmed as a white person would be. In relation to their respective population numbers, blacks are 10 times more likely to be shot and killed while unarmed as a white person would be.

Of all people shot and killed by police in 2015, 40% were black men, who only make up 6% of the total population. What is clear is that a disproportionate amount of blacks, men and women are killed then their population numbers would indicate. This is a problem. This is why a movement such as Black Lives Matters is needed to foster better training and better inter community relations in order to meet, debunk and socialise police officers to the black community. In my personal opinion, Blacks are demonized as dangerous criminals in the mind of law enforcement. Therefore, maximum precaution must be taken, and that action that done by a white person would be excused, done by someone who happens to have colour in their skin will result in a death sentence. By training officers better, familiarizing them with blacks who happen to be the most often target of black crime, police might build stronger community relations and bridge the gap to those communities. Also, this is not longer a desire, a request or an optional. All police need to have body cameras upon themselves. The camera never lies, and to show the public, what happened in the event of a police shooting will do wonders to help bridge the gap. Black people, just as white people, can see if an officer is in danger and forced to defend him or herself. It is the unknowing that causes the distrust. Show the videos fast and get them out into the media faster will prevent issues from arising in the communities affected in a police shooting. For when people can see the video, they can put themselves in the place of the police forced to kill someone. They will then make up their own mind if it was justified or not. Too often, those videos are held back cause mistrust, if the video cleared the officer why is it not being presented? There is also usually no good answer why there is a delay in showing the video.

Statistics are from; "Black Lives Matter vs. All Lives Matter Experiment DEBUNKED"

https://www.youtube.com/watch?v=voQ9BjnG5Cg

In Toronto

In Toronto, on Saturday, a teenager, hardly more than a boy, only 18 years old was shot and killed by police. Why is unknown at this time, but on the video 9 shots are fired at him. He was alone on a bus with a knife. Whose life were the police protecting? Perhaps they fired to stop him from cutting up those very special and expensive vinyl seats? We can only wonder when police were told to ignore common sense. The police were isolating the bus. The teenager was alone and the only danger was what he posed to himself. They would have had plenty of time to react if he tried to exit the bus. So why was there a hurry to take him down? Once contained inside the bus, they could have sat back and waited for health care professional, SWAT or someone,(anyone?), to come in and talk him down and out; to arrange for a non lethal reaction force; to do anything else other then shot and kill him. There is and must indeed be the case, that if no life is in danger, police do not fire their weapons. Period. When this simple rule was forgotten is anyone's guess

Are we to assume he was killed to protect himself from himself? What possible danger to anyone was he isolated and along on bus that was not moving? There were three bullets fired then a pause followed by 6 more. The boy fell down struck in the first fuselage. Why the additional 6 bullets? Where were they fired, at whom and where did they go? The simple fact is, those bullets were more of a danger to the community then any one with knife contained on a bus would ever be. Yet more questions to be answered which at this stage of the investigation, we have no answers for.

In Israel, where they have a clear and present danger of suicide bombers, they have a need for firing on sight. When security personnel see a person acting suspicious, dressed in bulky vests or jackets, acting suspicious and other signs of danger, they are to take the head shot if the person does not immediately obey orders to halt. Better one innocent dies than a suicide bomber killing many innocents that could have and should be prevented. Should we at least, not have the same level of protection here in Canada, where we do not have suicide bombers? Nor the need for swift action? Where it is more likely a mentally ill person will do themselves harm than will do harm to others? Should the police not have strict guidelines that say unless a life is in clear and present danger they do not use deadly force? And should they now all, immediately be retrained on this common sense rule?

There was no cause to fire a gun at that teenage Saturday night. There was no rush to resolve the situation. The scene was contained on the bus with no other innocents in danger. Common sense would have rewarded the city of Toronto, the province and even the country with a forgotten non story, if they had de-escalated the teenager and talked him out. Instead, there was no cause that this family must bury their child. In the family's press release, they call this a tragedy. Indeed, one that must be used to improve police services in Canada. Otherwise this poor child died in vain. Make his death meaningful so that the next time police face a mentally ill person who can do others no harm, they do not kill him when they should be there to protect him, from himself. They should be trained to not use their guns unless a life is in clear danger. With no one on that bus, who but the teen was in any danger?

Rhetoric of Hate

Does the rhetoric of Donald Trump rise to being hate speech? While what he is doing is in fact inciting hatred towards Muslims and Hispanics, he is not breaking any laws. He has just made it acceptable to go mainstream with his racism and not be shamed by the very public surrounding him for utter such garbage and filth. The only good thing about all of is this, with this increased attention upon the Muslim community, it has forced them to be more welcoming and hold outreach session to the community in order to broaden the public knowledge and understanding of who and what they are.

It is very hard to hard someone who happens to also be the doctor you trust... or the pharmacist. While Muslims make up 1% of the American population, they make up 2-10% of the doctors and pharmacist depending on methodology in the count. In any case a great percentage than their share of the population would account for. Thus far, the American Islamic community has been insular, keeping to themselves, Sheltered within its mosques. After 911, they went even further to hide from a very hostile community seeking to cast blame on anyone remotely associated with the terrorists. No matter how far a stretch to do so. Now, due to the political climate from such as Donald Trump, they have no choice but to come out of hiding. They have to branch out and make friends in the community. Make alliances with the people within their own community that they live in and make "Open Door" a policy for all to come, every day, not just by invitation or on special days.

A few things

A woman protesting on anti Muslim rally day... yes there is such a thing... Never underestimate man's ability to hate fellow man...

https://www.youtube.com/watch?v=to4U-09zkAw

She was outside a mosque and the cops were all in force to prevent trouble. She was out numbers by both cops as she was the only one to show up. And the evil Muslim came out and did what? They offered her what? Hatred for hatred? Evil for evil? No, they offered her tea and cookies, and then invited her inside. Surprisingly... she agreed and went.

Big deal, she is just one person; one heart, and one mind but with one person at a time. Next time someone tells her that Muslims are all evil, she will go... "Yes most of them... not all..." And that is a worthy start. One person at a time.

New York City, two cops sitting in their car, a 4x4 drives up and tosses in a bag, cop 1, Officer Peter Cybulski says "Boss it's a bomb." Cop 2, Sgt Hameed Armani, flicks on lights and sirens and gets out of 46th and Broadway (Time Square), so when the bomb goes off it would not kill hundreds of people...

https://www.youtube.com/watch?v=iaPV1hDyqcA

Turns out, the bomb was a dud. The suspect, I say with great surprise, (not) turns out to be mentally unstable in need of hospitalization. Cop 2, the driver, Sgt Hameed Armani, is a Muslim American from Afghanistan and a single father of a 12 year old daughter. He had ever reason to run from that bomb. Yet he did the one thing you could expect in the best of all of us. His duty. Nuff said. The two cops, one Christian, one Muslim, both prayed together as they drove like hell out of there. Now that was something more important, more profound and more importantly of all, it was more human than Donald trump will ever be with his hate filled rhetoric.

As well there was a knife attack in the London tube last year (December 6 2015) and the guy filming said clearly, "You aint no Muslim bro."

https://www.youtube.com/watch?v=IgNUwrIuihE

David Cameron then repeated that in the House of Commons and in a number of speeches.

https://www.youtube.com/watch?v=c5IxFNJNN5I

That one phrase did more to improve the vast perception of whom and what is a Muslim then anything that could have done or said. A Muslim man telling a knife wielding psychopath, you are not a Muslim! Short and sweet, yet cutting to the heart of this matter, it sums up what we should understand from this attack and this attacker. As that message passes from hand to hand and mouth to mouth, it resonates within the mind of the haters and those unsure. We knew that this sort of attack is done by the crazed, the insane and the mentally disturbed. Though they may shout some sort of religious slogan, "The devil can quote scriptures for his own end." They are not representative of any real Muslim group. Just those run of the mill haters of no worth to anyone. Just like Donald Trump is.

Police Chief Art Acevedo

art.acevedo@austintexas.gov

I would like to bring your attention to the video tape of Philip Turner from YouTube on Saturday night. (https://www.youtube.com/watch?v=iFxMnOmzGNw& sns=tw) Which you have called on your Twitter account to be: "Actions on this video aren't reflective of our policy or our values & are under investigation." These blatantly aggressive and frankly provocative actions on the part of both officers involved, particularly Officer Maufrais 7432, are nearing criminal in their outrageous conduct. While the video does not show any overly racist comments, those white officers all but acted in a racist fashion to African American Turner. However, unable to prove such an assumption, I would point out that there are grounds for a Federal lawsuit for acting under the colour of law, such as illegally issuing orders with regard to limiting his free movements and not allowing him to get to his car. Not to mention the blatantly violating Turner's rights to videotape the proceedings. Why did Officer Maufrais 7432 say that some of your officers were afraid of being photographed and recorded? Surely the only reason for such a fear would be if they were doing something wrong, as Officer Maufrais 7432 did on Saturday night. I would point out that in 19 out of 20 cases where police have been videotaped or used body cameras, police are exonerated by such recordings. These actions take on Saturday night should not be allowed to stand unchallenged. Swift follow up is needed by you and your department. Why? You have 5000 police officers at risk of being tarnished by the same brush of dishonourable conduct that this officer and his partner has done. Police are not above the law, not above department regulation. They are supposed to be guardians of the community not overlords to the inferior citizens. You have a city that is depending on you to lead your men and women to protect the city's good name, reputation and uphold the laws of the community, the state and the nation. Not create their own on the spot as they see fit to do on mere whim. Police have been the victims of bad press all over America this last year because of the actions of a few racists officers who had no business being on the force, let alone allowed to carry weapons capable of harming citizens. When I was a child, police where whom you turned to for help, not those you flee from as more dangerous than the criminals themselves, as is often the case with this bad press and poorer public relations. Building bridges, does not use Molotov cocktails to burn them down around us all. While I think this incident is minor, no one was hurt and no lasting damage has been done, if this is allowed to continue then what is next to happen? Just how out of control would Officer Maufrais 7432 be? False arrests? Physical assault? Or as we have seen on too many other videos, police officers illegally take human life without just cause? The city of Austin pays a salary to each officer to uphold the law. Can you honestly say those officers did so Saturday night? Whose law where they upholding? The police Department have internal policies, rules of conduct. Can you say with a straight face those offices acted within those guidelines or anywhere close to them? The US Constitution has the 1st Amendment allowing for the Freedom of the Press. Did your officers shower you, your police department and the City of Austin in the Great State of Texas of the United States of America by their actions this weekend to uphold this one citizen his right to be a citizen journalist? I would say they have not. My question thus can be put to you in a very simple fashion; what will you do about it as the leader, their commander and to whom the city has entrusted to lead their police force, make no mistake the police is owned, funded and fully under citizen control. What then will you do about this incident for it will be how the citizens judge you for your ability to uphold the law, their codes and their peace.

Flag Flap

Recently the American South has had to do some serious soul searching. A white man entered a black church killing nine men and women. The reaction was swift with the usual clamour for gun control, a dead issue, literally and figuratively in the U.S. But what did come of it was the flag, called the "Stars and Bars" that can be found on state flags and flying over the capital building. To some thinking, it is like the NAZI flag, a symbol of hate and slavery. The white oppression continues to this day and as such, it is time to come down. To others is means no such thing, but a symbol of the undying southern spirit of America. Historically, this flag was never the flag of the South, it was the battle standard. This distinction, while real, is of no matter, no real value is shown by this difference. It was flown in the Civil War. It is, as such, a part of the history of the South and can thus be claimed as such. After the war, all but forgotten, its use was revived by the Dixiecrats, a racist offshoot of the Democratic Party in 1948 with stated policy of non desegregation and opposition to granting the Afro-American full citizenship and equal rights. It was adopted on state flags as their battle flag, to say we are at war with the federal government, war with the blacks and at war with any attempt to allow people still living as little more than slaves to have the chance of becoming better off than they have been.

No one plays the villain in their own story. So father to son, mother to daughter, they never said we fly that flag so that Afro-Americans will know their place under the white man's boot, living in poverty and shame, without a chance to have their own part of the American dream. No, that sort of talk would make them the bad guys. Instead they retreated from history and reality into talking about patriotism, "Patriotism is the last refuge of a scoundrel," said Samuel Johnson. And here it comes. The flag was about Southern

Pride, and Southern Liberty and being of the South! It had nothing to do with Blacks, Afro-Americans, de-segregation, slavery or such like. Nope, the Stars and Bars is part of Southern heritage.

It has been almost 60 years since the days of the Dixiecrats. Now they are a boring subject best left and forgotten in the past for truly they are not who the South is, proclaims to be or even who they want to be. Over the last three or four generations, the people having been told this lie have come to accept is as if it were true. This flag is their symbol of their heritage of being from the South. Having become their symbol of Southern Pride and of their true Southern Heritage they see nothing derogatory of flying it proudly. The South was never defined by the slavery issue and racism. No matter how people try to box them in to that narrow definition. The Civil War was about states' rights, one of the important of said rights was slavery, but when 90% of your population did not own slaves, only the very rich did, you would never get them to rally to an issue that did not affect them. So the Civil War was framed to be about state's rights. Just as today, there are still racists running around the South and the ever haunting KKK, they are on the fringe of society. As one of the friends of the accused in the church shooting said, paraphrasing, "We knew he was a racist and we knew he was crazy, what we did not know was that he was that racist and that crazy."

Today, removing the Stars and Bars is not about losing a part of their heritage, it is about reclaiming their true heritage. The South has always been an open, welcoming, friendly place. That flag has turned from the symbol of hate to the heritage of the south and Southern Pride.

So when you hear people supporting the flag Stars and Bars, they may not be racists at all. So don't hate, instead explain and relate. It is for this very reason that the flag must come down. Because of its history of hatred, it blocks the true South heritage of neighbourly people trying to get along with everyone. While the flag is a small part of the heritage, it is blocking the Sunlight shining on the even more important and more welcoming, true spirit of Southern Heritage; their pride in being tolerant and open to new people, new ideas and accepting them for who and what they are. Judging by the content of their character, not the colour of their skin, or the flag they fly.

Latina and Latino

The so called illegal immigration issue in the USA has reached the point where stupidity is rampant. To wit, the Republicans are going to end birthright citizenship, guaranteed under Article 14 of the Bill of Rights. This argument has even gone to the point where a radio shock jock is calling for all Illegal's to be made slaves. How did that work out again President Lincoln? This issue is at best silly and worst outright dangerous. However, despite the equally silly lack of response from the few who are paying any attention to this, what is missed is the reason. Yes, there is a reason, a secret toy surprise in this Grand Old Party box of crack Jacks. Why are they calling for this war upon illegal immigrants? Donald trump calls them rapists, drug dealers and worse. From whence comes this vitriol?

Hispanics, mostly from Mexico but from Latin America are about to become the largest minority. With the projected increase in population, Latino's will go from being around the same amount but slightly larger than as blacks to triple in size.

"The Latino population, already the nation's largest minority group, will triple in size and will account for most of the nation's population growth from 2005 through 2050. Hispanics will make up 29% of the U.S. population in 2050, compared with 14% in 2005."

"http://www.pewsocialtrends.org/2008/02/11/us -population-projections-2005-2050/"

"Across all nationality groups except Cubans, the Democratic advantage in party identification among Latinos is greater than 20 percentage points, and this is true across nearly all states. Even among Cuban-Americans, the once large GOP lead has dwindled to just six percentage points."

"http://cis.org/RepublicanEffortAttractLatinoVoters"

Essential, what we are seeing is this; the increase in Latinos will result in the number of voters for the democratic candidates increasing as the share of republicans decreases.

Republicans, especially with those who self identify with the "Tea Party Movement", are forced to gerrymander their electoral districts to even have any chance of being elected. As such, over time the number of elected people identifying in their cohort will shrink as their voter support shrinks.

Lastly, by emphasizing the deportation of "Others", in this case Latinos, they allow a forthright excuse to discriminate against a large minority group within main stream politics and media.

During the height of the "Potato Famine" of Ireland, it was not uncommon to see signs posted, "Help wanted - No Irish Need Apply". Today it is not enough to say, no Gays need be married, despite the Supreme Court ruling! No the Republicans have to all but demand that the Constitution be scrapped in favor of their own limited re-election hopes and to hell with even the semblance of democracy. "One person, one vote" should now read, "One white male, heterosexual with strong Tea Party leanings, One vote." I was go to conclude with a comment of just how un-American this type of political position is, to treat others as less than full citizens but then I realized, of course, it is just as American to in fact do so.

"Article I, Section 2 read's, "Representatives and direct Taxes shall be apportioned among the several States which may be included within this Union, according to their respective Numbers, which shall be determined by adding to the whole Number of free Persons, including those bound to Service for a

Term of Years, and excluding Indians not taxed, three fifths of all other Persons."

Plus sa change, plus la meme

The more things change, the more they remain the same.

Why I am not a Feminist

This would be why I am not a feminist. "When you're young, you're thinking: 'Where are the boys? The boys are with Bernie,' " Ms. Gloria Steinem stated thusly an interview with the talk show host Bill Maher. This is a feminist icon? In effect she has just labelled all women as hormonal sex objects in their quest for males. I wonder just how far that is from say; "What she wearing, she was asking for it!" The problem is that with most good ideas, they become institutionalised that are turned into ideologies. Those ideologies become intolerant of anyone who does not follow the most bigoted of paths according to the likes of some unnamed but all powerful cabal of haters, utter their pearls of wisdom as if handed down from Mt Sinai, similar to what Steinem has said above. In an effort to distance themselves from each other, "Oh were not like that..." Feminist theory have sub divided the ideology of feminism into theories, many, up to 6 different so called "waves." As if, this makes a difference. "OH no, that is a femnazi, she is only a lipstick lesbian..." Err say what? Those are two different categories of feminism. No, the problem with being a "Feminist" is this; just like all Muslims are expect to apologise for all attack by terrorists no matter who or where they are, as if they were all close friends with any terrorist who raised a gun in the name of their prophet. All "Feminists" are merely considered the extension of worst offenders in their demand for ideological purity. This is the 21 century; does any rational human being disagree with the idea of equal pay for equal work? Note Donald J trump does. But I repeat, I did say any RATIONAL human being. Thereby the Donald does not qualify. Enraging your audience with a term, "Feminism" that no one understands, (including those who seemingly must divide it into waves in the first place,) but everyone gets leery of, defeats the purpose. The real reason I am not a feminist can be seen as originally stated by Simone de Beauvoir; paraphrased thusly: "The point is not change names, the point is to change things for the better." Feminism is dead! Long live equality for all, men, women, LBGT. People of world can get behind that phrase a lot easier than they ever will to get behind hateful, utterance of a so call feminist icon like Gloria Steinem. Oliver Cromwell had this to say to her likes; "You have sat too long for any good you have been doing lately... Depart, I say; and let us have done with you. In the name of God, go! (Address to the Rump Parliament)" I say to you Gloria Steinman, "Go now, you have staid too long atop that throne of false lives and thin veneer of contempt for other women. You are no friend to females as you pretend to be. Depart, I say; and let us have done with you and your tired old hatred of men and women who yearn to breathe their own free air, of their own free will, who won't follow along your ideological path to oblivion." That is why I am not a feminist.

Transgender

North Carolina deserves a note of thanks! Not for passing a discriminatory bill against transgender people but for opening that whole discussion to the national political stage and international reflection. We can ask ourselves just what is their problem with regulating bathrooms in the South? You would think they would have better things to do? I think this is a happy time! It really is. Look at the history of discrimination in the South. First there was Slavery. This caused the American Civil War and when civil rights won out, Amendments were made to the constitution. The result was Jim Crow laws. Complete with separate bathrooms, separate but equal no doubt. The answer was civil right legislation. Being unable to discriminate against blacks any more, they switch to gays and lesbians. Again the Supreme Court crushed there laws on discrimination. So now they are reduced to regulating who stand up to pee and who sits down? Perhaps we should simple rename this as #pee-gate.

Being transgender is not simple guys dressing in drag. It is a lot more involved and a lot more complicated. Starting at a very young age, perhaps before the age of 2, GTM, Girls to Men, MTG, Men to Girls, before they can even think of themselves as having a sexual identity, start to act out in such a way as to portray themselves as the opposite of social norms society has assigned for their biological gender. Thus when they can articulate for themselves, they will assert they are in fact in opposition to that biological destiny assigned by society. They will think of themselves as the other sex and act accordingly. Thus leading to a lifetime of conflict with social normative views and sadly being outcasts from what we expect a little boy or little girl to be and to act. This growing up they struggle with the overwhelming message sent by society to behave according to script on the one hand

and yet their inner need to be true to themselves. Nietzsche, perhaps out of context did offer the answer. "Become who you are." Today, we live in a more open and understanding society, North Carolina notwithstanding, that people who are transgender are given a more accepting and welcoming transition. Laws still need to be enacted and amended in order to ensure the safety and protection from discrimination for transgender people. But as with the Stonewall Riots that forced society to confront the lesbian and gay community. North Carolina will force society to now confront transgender people.

The reason why people can think that Transgender are some sort of pervert waiting to rape little girls in bathrooms, (seemingly rape, molestation and assault are still against the law in North Caroline? What need is there to add another law on top of those, if not to merely discriminate against an undefined but clearly in need of protection minority group?) Is because they do not know who or what a transgender person is. In order to help you, and myself, I went to YouTube to find transgender peoples who could explain who they are.

I don't think you need agree with everything they say, or even find all their content to be universally enjoyable, to find that after only a few minutes watching that these ladies are smart, articulate and above all else, human beings worthy of our respect and admiration for showing the straight world who they are but also granting us a view with these small slice of their world.

Be they smart, funny or beautiful, they do not ask your permission to be who they are, they, in the immortal words of Marin Luther King, "They shall overcome!"

Maya

https://www.youtube.com/channel/UCf0CRezZ YOUcvqrdMmozowQ

Brittney Kade

https://www.youtube.com/channel/UCcKor6He 5ZbTUYlvNntcEmw

PRINCESSJOULES

https://www.youtube.com/channel/UCT9IRRTB WlqMlfVgSyfsg7Q

Transgender a Follow up

#Pee-gate Part Two

This gift keeps on giving...

In my recent blog, I posted about North Carolina and their law banning transgender people from going to their self selected bathroom, forcing them instead to the bathroom of their biological identity. In reaction, many videos have surfaced showing the results of this open display of ignorance at best and sheer discrimination at worst. I would like to review three of them that caught my eye. First video (Linked below), taken in December, (2015?) surfaced showing police demanding identification from a lesbian woman deemed by said police to be not worthy of being female based on her looks, to being allowed into a female bathroom. When she refused, not having any, she is escorted out of the bathroom, insultingly called "Sir" by the police. (Who carried ID to the bathroom?)Now we can see future fall out, women will need to carry and show ID to law enforcement be allowed into bathrooms. Those without will be removed as a danger to society. Luckily, and surprisingly, no lasting damage or assault by the self righteous police officer was done even as they were rough in their handling of her for attempting to illegally pee... Wait, I am sure that there will be forthcoming future assaults. But things get worse.

We turn to our second video, where a black man, who sounded on the video to be foreign, perhaps poor sound quality, made me think he was African? Hence, my use of his racial identity in this description. Specifically, my thought was he sounded foreign? Maybe he is from Uganda; the country that outlawed being Homosexual by putting them to death, and thereby explaining why he was so hyper alert? In any case, this man follows a woman into the bathroom because he felt she was not female enough. So we may see in such a short time, what an accomplishment this new law in South Carolina has done. Not only does it bar transgender from using the bathrooms, but we may now morally discriminate against women born as women, using the women's bathroom, if we self select that they are not feminine enough for out liking, even to the point where police can now throw them out for such offending individuals and call them "Sir" just to be on the safe side from any potential lawsuit or other legal ramifications if they fail to produce gender identification sufficient to police.

Our last video, to which I will not link; for any publicity might earn him YouTube money, is I would have hoped inspired by bad comedy, long since past any point of being humorous. A bad joke doing in an attempt to make light of this clearly outrageous law... I seem to recall a similar skit from the Garry Shandling show, going along the same lines but I could be wrong as it was so long ago. In any case, a man does a "social experiment" to see just what happens when a male enters a female bathroom, much to amusement of viewers? So wearing a dress, makeup and a wig, cameras rolling, he enters a female bathroom. Only to be told to leave repeatedly by different women, even as he explained that he was transgender and just trying to use the washroom. One can see the comedy potential here right? The thing I forgot to mention? He had a full beard, a face full of facial hair. Haw haw, yuck yuck. Clearly this is comedy right? The saddest part of all? Is that this is not the comedy channel but a serious political commentary. This guy actually thinks this is his exposing the transgender "lies" for what they are. Showing the justification for such a law and why it is needed. As if a man transiting to female would not shave, or a female transiting to male would wear wigs, dresses and makeup with a beard. Yet this is the level of sophistication for the supporter of the anti transgender bathroom law from North Carolina. Is it any wonder why this law gives rise to a new level of hatred toward anyone differing from normative values of self imposed white male politicians? This law not only allows for open discrimination against Trans people, it now allows for misogyny to show open contempt for women and misogynists be openly critical or women's dress habits, even up to police intervention. Recall in the first video, how the police called the lady "Sir" to further humiliate and demean her and her sex. She is not following their normative in wear, or makeup and thus must harassed, humiliated and treated like a criminal, all for going to the bathroom. This is the real legacy of North Carolina. Congratulations; this is surely something to be proud of! In one foul (sic) swoop, not only do they demean a minority group, they put all women on notice, there is now a bathroom dress code. And the Police are now ready to enforce it. But they now have opened the door to outright hostility towards anyone not living up to the expectations of what a woman should wear and look like.

Lesbian evicted from bathroom

https://www.youtube.com/watch?v=hVuHAS2CtUM

Women's Bathroom Patrolled by man

https://www.youtube.com/watch?v=dMA0mTPul-g (Video has since been removed)

Transgender Part Three

Pee-gate part three

First, the good news: the Trudeau government plans to introduce legislation next week that will allow for Trans people to be protected under discrimination laws, and bars people from discriminating against them. As well, they will be adding them specifically to the groups protected under hate legislation. While this is long overdue, the ideological hatred of the so called conservative right for anyone not fit into their Neo Con mold, left this group of Canadians literally out in the cold. So far, so good! We await the specifics of the bill, but they tend to leak it for public review prior to actually releasing it. So it should go over well. Since the Liberals have a majority and they will be supported by the NDP so this bill should pass quickly with little opposition from the Conservative Reform Alliance Party. Canada thus is perusing Wales to have the best legislative protection for all members of our society and including the Trans people within out umbrella of protected rights, Wales being the first country to enact such legislative protection for Tran's people. This is a trend we would very much like to see exported, adopted and duplicated around the world. The next new item would be the opposite, something not to be exported, not to be adopted and hopefully, never more to be duplicated around the world.

Having said the good stuff, let's turn to the bad side of things. In the state of North Carolina, rather than accept they made a mistake, and change their anti Trans law, double downed on this issue. They filed suit against the US Government, who in turn quickly filed suits against the state. So now this is in the hands of the judiciary, where we have seen just recently that they can in fact be trusted to come down on the progressive side of human rights issues.

But wait! It gets worse! Republican Lt. Gov. Dan Patrick stated this week that Texas would rather forgo billions of dollars, likely to be around 10 billion dollars, in Federal education grants rather than be forced not to discriminate against teenagers. Now even if you are stupid, 10 billion dollars is more than pocket change. But to present ideological unity and to suppress the rights of as many 13 000 Tran's students in Texas schools, the Lt Governor will toss out 10 billion dollars. Where that money then will come from is unknown. But as education is not on the list of importance for Republicans they may just as well not replace it. After all, they have no education and look how they turned out; mean spirited religious bigots. Heck everyone should be entitled to be that insane. 10 billion dollars over which bathroom a few people will use? Now that is hardcore ideology. For people who claim to be strong supporters of the Constitution, they read the 2nd Amendment and forgo the rest. Like the Supremacy clause (Article VI, Clause 2) that allows the Federal Government to set the minimum standards for things. You can do more but never less. When there is conflict between federal and state law, whereas the federal law says more is to be done and the state law mandates for less, the federal law must be supreme and be the only law allowed to carry the day. SO the states can do more, imagine just for an instant, the bigot stats doing their job and shaming the federal government into being progressive? What a fine day that would be.

At what point will someone walk up and say; "Stop"? There are real issues to be dealt with, important issues to deal with. This is not one of them. This is the question of who goes to what bathroom. And yet more money will be spent on this issue that could be spent on real issues, health care, education... oh wait Texas will forgo education grants... The face of ideological hatred is scary. With no claim to reason, they will literally cut their nose to spit their face just because they would rather be hateful then be reasonable. At what point along the lines of 10 billion dollars do we pause just for a second to ask, well is this so bad? To allow teenagers in school to be accommodated and allowed to go to the bathroom that they identify with?

Free Speech and Transgender

Recently, the Federal government introduced C-16, an act to amend the Human Code to add in to the protected classes, transgender, such that it will protect transgender persons from being discriminated upon. As well as adding this to the legislation for hates crimes. Something that made me feel proud to be Canadian. Helping these small minority groups be protected whereas in the United States they are looking for legislation to discriminate against them. So this was all good and great until it came to my attention that people were protesting this new bill. I was shocked yet intrigued to why they were upset. So of course, I studied their arguments. I found them to have one. This was a matter of free speech. They held that this new bill would curtail their freedom of speech in the things they were allowed to say. They are, of course, right in that. It is a limit on what can and should not be said. I waited for them to continue with more. Only there was no more to be had. This was their argument. The bill placed a limit on free speech and thus should be opposed. At which point, I understood all I need to know, which is, they do not understand free speech, freedom and or Canada. Said to say, but let me enlighten them upon this. The freedom of speech has always been to protect without limits the parts of speech that were political. So if the government passed a law saying that you cannot vote for party X then that would be a violation. Advertisers cannot lie to you in their ads and claim they have free speech. You cannot go into a crowded theater and start to scream "Fire!" Yet both of the latter two examples are speech that is curtailed. Why? Because the notion of free speech is not without its limits, and in this case, C-16 imposing rather limited extensions of speech. Not that this will stop conversation, or limit politic discussions. It will limit hate speech. Can we agree that hating is not speech we want to protect or even allow? Einstein did not write "E=mc^2, and die transgender die!" Why? It is because his argument only needed to rest on the physics of the matter, the science of this discovery, and upon the ideas themselves that needed no further elaboration. Sir Arthur Eddington who then was the first man to prove Relativity, happened to be gay, yet at no time did he mention that as part of his proof for major discovery at the turn of the last century. So then why should we allow for anything of the sort that we call protected classes to enter when discussing any issue. We limit hate speech because it is inherently not political; it is inherently not part of any discussion. It is an end to political speeches to gather support with arguments and words and the beginning of the call to violence, both verbal and sadly physical. Hate speech is a call to violence and attacks upon the person. So yes, C-16 does limit free speech, but is a narrowly construed limit that does not interfere with legitimate political speech. So the argument opposing C-16 on the grounds of free speech does not have merit. Freedom of speech is to be able to freely discuss ideas, not to be the siren song for discrimination. C-16 is a good law that needs to be enacted to protect a minority subject to violence and discrimination. Which is why we have subject classes in the first place, to protect minorities that have been discriminated upon in the past, but hopefully not into our future.

Bathroom Guardians

In other news this week, a lady entering a female bathroom was stopped by a security guard and forcible removed from the grocery store because the guard felt that she was not female enough to use the bathroom of her choice. Yes, she was transgender but this was in New York not North Carolina. Police were called and arrested the security guard for assault and hate crimes. This event calls to mind a YouTube's "social experiment" of a man wearing a dress and makeup entering a series of women's bathrooms with a beard. See how funny that is? And can you see the humor in the latest event? See the lady got assaulted, see funny that is? See the guard go to jail for up to 5 years for assault and addition 5 years for a hate crime, if found guilty? Come on, where your sense of humour? Hat is so funny... Oh wait, sorry, none of this is funny. Not the assault, not the social experiment humour. None of it. Because someone, a real person, who just had to use the bathroom, was humiliated and denied service as ever other person would be allowed to use, all because someone felt they had the right to pick on a weaker, smaller, minority group, seen as out of favour by the majority of bigots and transphobes. The people who find this type of humor funny are also going to find it hilarious for a bunch of men to don white sheets and plant a burning cross on the lawn of a black family. And then find it outrageous to be connected to a small, pathetic, mentally unstable man who walked into a black church and kills all the people inside praying. Hate is hate. You can try to call it humour but people will see right through that and know you are nothing more than a pathetic passive aggressive wanna-be who has failed at being anything other than just mean.

For Shame

With a cry of "None is too many," Barry Wilson in his best, "let me be the reasonable xenophobic" voice to channel his inner American Republican Presidential candidate in an ill-informed, clearly insulting and absolutely a disservice to his viewership. The Trudeau plan to bring in so many refuges is a humanitarian gesture, long overdue for those suffering, first from the ISIS terrorist establishment, then the long journey to freedom into mainland Europe, and now the long cold winter. Speed is of the urgency. Get those people here, where they too can be safe from terrorists, establish a new home and be warm from the winter, where they too can be forced to listen to Barry Wilson's poorly thought out excuses for editorials.

Mr. Wilson, should stick to his regular insult to the intelligence of the audience and not try to surpass himself with this latest editorial. None is too many is reference to the same sort of self assured xenophobic rants aimed at the Jews as they fled the NAZI's of Germany seek to find a new home; "What's the rush? You are exaggerating, things are not that bad," as they were lead, in file, to the death camps. In the ensuing 80 years, have we learned nothing? For shame, Barry Wilson, for shame!

When we forget our humanity and duty towards suffering souls, we have not merely allowed the terrorism of extremists to win; we have invited them to take control of our agenda.

Swedish Meat Ball

A new law in Sweden proposes that a man may opt out of being a father in the same way a woman having an abortion might do so and opt out of having a child. The man before the 18th week of gestation can vote to terminate all of his parental rights to the child and forgo any other privileges in being the mere sperm donor to that child. This is in effect the male abortion bill. The man would no longer be responsible or have any parental or legal input to the child's life. This sounds like a fair proposal for the man, who no longer would be liable for child support, parent responsibility or even simple affection for said child, the fruit of his loon. Sounds like a win, err, no not a win-win, but more like a win-"go fuck yourself." The woman has an absolute right to an abortion before the fetus is viable. Until a fetus is viable, it is not a person and as such abortion is universally allowed in most states and countries. This is biology. However at some point the women must either accept or prevent the pregnancy. The man has the absolute right to be responsible and wear protection before impregnating the women. The normally resulting condition from such behavior is having babies? The man has to prevent it before hand. Otherwise they are stuck with the bill. Except for a few things; what about the child? Where do their rights fit in? What about the child in question, produced by the act or acts of irresponsibility by the couple and then further betrayed by the state to allow for yet another act of take no responsibility? What about that child, forgotten in the shame of standing up for the male and being fair.

Many children living in poverty are there because of one parent families. Mostly, the father having absconded and forgone, child support , a duty of love and care, and just being there for the child as they grow to adulthood. The child has a right to know the other side, i.e. the father's side, as in who they are and where did they come from. Claiming this is not fair to the man, considered an adult in such matters, the women may always abort is her slice of fairness. The man is without options under current law. This neatly forgets the man had all the freedom in the world to wear the condom in the first place. Why then is the disproportionate burden thrust upon the male to provide for an unwanted child without any say in the matter upon conception? Even if said child may be force to grow up in poverty, in an emotion desert, wondering why they were abandoned in the first place, what had they done to deserve such a fate? Who is equally thusly deprived of their father emotional support, legally, by law? Such an act by the government betrays the child in favour of irresponsibility. If a man, wishing to not be burdened by parental responsibility, they then have the sole responsibility to wear a condom. Something rather simple to do, especially considered in light of the burden they force the child into a life time of living. For the state to pass such a law, allowing for such male abortion, then the state must ensure that there is no child poverty, unlimited access to psychological support, and generally impose an additional burden on the clearly shrinking moral, responsible adults within society to yet again take care of the legal cast off by an irresponsible state.

4. Other Subjects

Je Suis Charlie

Dateline early January 2015

"But whoever earns an offense or a sin and then blames it on an innocent [person] has taken upon himself a slander and manifest sin."

Surat An-Nisa' 4:112

"Have you killed an innocent person who had killed none? Verily, you have committed a thing "Nukra" (a great Munkar - prohibited, evil, dreadful thing)!"

Surat Al-Kahf 18:74

In the late morning, Paris time, Gunfire broke out in the offices of Charlie Hebdo. Two armed attackers had killed so many people inside while claiming to have avenged the Prophet Mohammed in this act. In the past, this satirical magazine had poked fun at the Prophet and at Islam. The ongoing further events need not concern us here. Who and why are not for us to judge. We have in two short sentences enough information to reach our goal of a better understanding of Islam and the enemies of God, Allah and the Prophet Mohammed. First, let us assume that the editors had in fact insulted the Prophet and thus was deserving of punishment. Allah is a just God but he is patient and it is his right to reward his followers as well to punish the wicked. It is for him and him alone, when to exact his just punishment from them for their wickedness. So then with their untimely death at the hand of the gunmen, they became the victim. Allah being just cannot punish the innocent, as he would like, Allah is a just God, thus he must offer them succour for their wickedness done onto them. Thus instead of the punishment they had earned with their cartoons, he would have to offer them comfort for having been unjustly murdered. Thus Allah, has had his will thwarted and his justice denied by those gunmen.

Who then could have dared do this to Allah? While in Paris, CSI comb for ever clue, picking up all evidence, Allah is all knowing. He knew who has committed this wickedness. He knows why they have done so, for he knows all that is in their heart. They were not trying to be the true followers of Allah. They were usurping the right of this jealous God to punish the wickedness of men with divine justice. Not mortal vengeance, but absolute eternal justice, that only Allah can meet out.

As such, those two misguided fools have case themselves into the burning fires of hell. They have not served Allah; they have taken upon themselves to meet out the divine justice of Allah as if this God was not a God but a mere name, a word, a boogie man to scare little children with. So who is the disbeliever deserving of punishment? Who are the innocent, cut down before it was Allah's will to do so?

In the Holy Book of the Jews, Christians and Muslims, they tell a story of Abraham and his son Isaac. The Jews and Christians say that Abraham was ordered by God to take his son and kill him for God. The age of the child is never mentioned from that of a baby to an adult male, while it is easy to kill a baby in diaper, the obedience to God is better seen if he, the son, is a man. As Abraham drove the blade at the chest of the son, the angel of the Lord stopped him and saved the child's life. The Qur'an says this is a wicked deed and the dream telling Abraham to kill his son was sent by the devil to trick him. This is why the angel of the lord had to stop him.

The next time, a true follower of Allah is told to kill anyone in the name of Allah for some crime against Allah, remember this story of Charlie Hebdo, and the Qur'an. For in them you will have your answer. It was wicked to kill those people. It is wicked to take the place of Allah. And by doing this wickedness, you are taking upon yourself the sin of others and must pay for their crimes with your eternal life.

In Baghdad, Iraq, in order to fool security forces, two retarded children, aged 11 and 13, were kidnapped and put in a car bomb. No one would ever think to look in such a car with two very innocent little girls in it. As the driver fled on foot, the bomb exploded killing many in the market place including those intellectually challenged little girls. When faced with such a thing, can we all agree, Jew, Christine and Muslim, that this is an evil act? For if we cannot, then this world is already in a hell, no God would be cruel enough to make themselves.

Ottawa Shooting

It has been the sort of week that demands reflection. Not one but two good men were cut down for any other reason than to doing their duty. The first, run down for daring to wear his uniform to get a coffee. Injuring a second man in the process, who will live. Sparking a second even more vicious attack, that ended with a Hollywood style leap into the air, twist and firing before Kevin Vickers landed to kill the suspect, worthy of John McCain of Die Hard fame. And all the praise thus forth received. Why did he feel such a need to risk his own life? In past times, they would have waited for surrender, but a suicide vest and he would take out half of the house of Parliament. The Threat had to be stopped at any cost. Another man, and his team, who risked their lives to save others. Sadly the first man, doing his duty, was not so lucky.

At the Ottawa War Memorial, Cpl. Nathan Cirillo was shot in the back and killed in a cowardly ambush. Let us shed no tear for him, he would ask for none but let us offer all praise and celebrate him and his life of duty. For this was what he wanted to do. What he was most proud of doing, and to his end, he died doing his duty. Guarding fallen comrades that he would all too soon join was his post. He stood his post to the last. When told he was selected to be there, I am very sure, that he leaped for joy, this is the kind of duty that is given only to the best of the best. Getting it, said in the eyes of his superiors, he was worthy of such an assignment. Basically getting the military gold medal. An honour in itself to be selected to serve in this fashion, to guard, all compete fiercely for the honour. Yet with all duty, they bring a burden. His post was to guard and so he did, to the end of his life. A life now fitting to be the first name added to our Hall of Hero's, where his gunman met his end, not soon enough for Cpl. Nathan Cirillo, but his end did come.

The assailant, Michael Zahaf-Bibeau, bipolar, self medicating his condition with drugs saw the earlier events and snapped. He was not getting help or treatment so he would force them to treat him. In a very destructive version of a child acting out, one man was killed and a nation in shock. Yet some conclusion must be drawn.

First, in what can only be seen as the greatest irony since John Lennon, "Happiness is a warm gun" was killed by said gun violence. The open question is where did he get such a weapon as the long gun he carried? The irony is that the answer might well be in the long gun registry abolished by the same government that he may have been trying to kill.

ISIL, the Islamic State of Iraq and the Levant claimed him as their revenge. So as I understand they wish to send bipolar, self medicating druggies, to ambush and back shoot in the most cowardly of ways as their harbinger of vengeance? I suspect that says more about their methods and organization then anything about Canada.

Lastly, the repercussions of it all upon our nation. First, all the grand theater and Churchillian Rhetoric, "We shall stand on the back bencher's, we shall stand in the Red Room, We shall never surrender," left aside. This was no attack upon Canada. This was no vengeance mission from a far off place. This was merely a tragedy for all involved. Keven Vickers took a life. Never a burden one would want to carry. Cpl. Nathan Cirillo killed before his life could fulfill its promising start and last Michael Zahaf-Bibeau, a life devastated from his start by his malfunctioning mind.

The Canadian military has ordered that no persons should wear uniform unless on official business, to prevent further attacks. Uniformly, (SIC) they have obeyed their orders but expressed defiance of it.

So I declare that this Remembrance Day, November 11, 2014, all people wear Camouflage of any sort to say, we will not be cowed, we will not run, and we will not be intimidated.

_____

Lone Wolf

The question presented after last week's tragedy, must be how to prevent it in future. The Prime Minister feels that additional power to security services and arming CSIS, (Canadian Security Intelligence Service) is the right way to go. For the fear is not that other groups will infiltrate and act in a mass assault, but single, one person sprees of violence will occur. Similar in nature to both of last week events, but echoed around the world. Such as an ax welding maniac attacked to police in New York City, or the school shooting on the Left Coast or any number of previous such innocents. Even the FBI is claiming that such events are on the increase. Sadly read the news paper and it is true, there is no escaping the problem. There is also, to date, no effort to understand the problem either. Thus far, the issue has been that of law enforcement, bravado and big speeches of "We shall fight them on the beaches" not seeking solutions or even answers except in that narrow focus. All of which grab headlines and fuel ratings. They do nothing to sort out and solve the problem. And until they do, you can be sure more and more such incidents will occur. And no amount of new powers or adding weaponry to any agency will curtail or stop.

It earns votes for a politician to be tough on crime, and promise more punishment and better service to protect people. The TV stations love such events; they cancel programming and go straight to on the scene of the events. "Live" as the manhunt continues. Report rumour and events as fast as things occur, glue viewership to their screens and radios all day. Even the average citizen, seeing such events, root for the good guys to catch the evil doer and then demand extreme forms of punishment for said entertainment. Sadly, this is nothing more than a modern day Inquisition, to ferret out the false evil doings and bring them to God's Judgment, (as is she needed any help to do that) only now they can win the ratings war or get re-elected to boot. Win, win for all concerned. Except for all the people hurt. The killer is killed, His victim is dead, and at least one man shall burden his soul with the taking of a human life, no matter how legitimate, and necessary it is, it shall always remain a burden that will wake him at night. Oh and the self radicalization? Happens not in some dark room with voices from hell? No, it happens on TV, right in the same living room. These people are using ad hoc weapons they have access to and going wild from what they see on TV and movies. If the lone wolf is at this point where TV is going to generate their copy cat attack, then we have already failed them.

So then what the solution? It is not sexy and won't win any votes, ratings or anything but it will solve the problem. The lone wolf is not alone. They are in the community and with a little help from government using scarce tax payer resources could provide additional medical help and intervention, as well as counselling and crisis centers, we could take care of most of the mental health issues. In fact, the more of these events, the more, the common denominator is the person was bipolar. Their break from reality while, tragic, is entirely predictable and treatable with the right training and resources. Mental illness however is a taboo topic, shunted to the side and left in the closet rather than front and center to help solve the problem. This is a medical health issue, not law and order. We need Dr. Kildare, Marcus Welby, M.D. and Dr Mark Green not Rambo, James Bond or Joe Friday.

Medical treatment would uncover the lone wolf before they grow teeth, and proper treatment would remove them from the path to radicalisation simply by treating the underlying issue. By offering treatment not judgment, the people who might "go off" like a destructive whirlwinds, may be prevented from their insanity, thus saving lives in the long run including their own. But sadly, present government efforts are not geared to help solve the problem; it is about new powers to police, guns for CSIS, re-election of government, and TV ratings.

Response one (Thanks M)

So many Lone Wolfs are not necessarily mentally ill as much as they are "Outcasts" from society. They do not fit in so it must be the existing society that is at fault, not them. A poor mindset is not mental illness as currently defined and not treatable.

From Norway, Anders Behring Breivik (Norwegian greatest mass killer ruled insane) to the Unabomber, Ted Kaczynski, to nearly all the other people, lone wolves in the headline news, they all show symptoms of being bipolar, and in fact many have been seeking treatment, had treatment or even in treatment. The first thing that comes to mind when you hear of such an attack is, "that guy is crazy" and in fact that is where we need to deal with this problem. Not that they are outcasts but why they feel this way. Once they become a police issue, it is too late! There is a crime done, someone is hurt or property damage. If we can take care of the mental health problems and keep in on that level, then we eliminate 85-90% of the lone wolves, a good first step. If we arm police more... what good is two pistols per cop, isn't one enough? And isn't their response is only after the grenade went off? A doctor with medication, need not wait for anything to go off, but ask any of them; they need more people, more resources, and more money... you can spend that tax dollar only once, the cops already have the guns and have failed thus far. Not for want of trying, but a failure to grasp the scope of the problem. Let's try something new. It may not help but we will not be repeating the same experiment over again, which is Einstein's definition of insanity.

Response 2 (Thanks F)

The many events with the U.S. Postal Service which they coined the phrase of "going postal" ... include the Oklahoma Massacre by or the Columbine shootings, the Sandy Hook shooting etc. The list goes on. Where it stops, no one knows, but clearly more bad law won't help, since the many laws we have now are not able to help. "Let's try something new. It may not help but we will not be repeating the same experiment over again, which is Einstein's definition of insanity."

Conspiracy? Nuts.

After 15 years of await for answers from the 9-11 hijacking terrorist attack, it seems then as now, merely asking questions results in cries of "Conspiracy nuts". Well I beg to differ, as such I offer you five questions, Who, What, When where and why of the 9-11 Terrorist Attack.

1) Who? Who were the hijackers? We have their names from the manifest; we have in one case, a passport that escaped the destruction of the plane. No conspiracy here, stand things like that just happen in real life that is simply beyond imagination. Yet we do not know who they were. All of the people in the manifest, or at least the names on their passports, have turned up alive and well in the Arabic world with the strangely similar tale of losing their passport to it was stolen. Not to mention the names are fairly common. Fair enough, then who were the hijackers?

2) What? What where they doing on the planes. The reason we know the name of the hijackers is because in 2000 the Millennial Bomber was caught coming over the border from Canada with the intent of attacking the West Coast. In the evidence gathered from his car was a list of names. The same names appeared on the flight manifest of the 9-11 planes. So what were they doing on a plane when their names should have been on a no fly list? There should have been some sort of warning built into the system? As if, hey we have all these names on a flight should we call security? George W. Bush, President did not want an investigation into the events, but even a simple car accident will get one from either the insurance company or the police, or both. We use investigations to find out what went wrong and more importantly to fix it. So what went wrong?

3) When? When was the planning done for the NORAD test that involved hijacked planes on the

American East coast being used to attack civilian targets? And did they use the TV Show 'The Lone Gunmen' pilot episode play a part in the planning of this scenario. Or perhaps better put, where did they plan to stage a drill on 9-9-9 in London. England UK involving three bombs in the 'Tube', their subway, and on a bus? Or yet again, the planning for the Oklahoma City Bombing, where ATF agents were drilling on scenario of a car bomb in front of a federal building set to explode. One is a surprising coincidence. But by round three if you are not scratching your head going, "Boy is that weird." So again, we must ask when where these drills planned and who knew about them?

4) Where? Where are the tapes for the Pentagon cameras? All told it is rumored that some 87 cameras were able to capture some or all of the attack on the Pentagon that morning. Including the gas station right across from where the plane hit. Immediately after the attack, agents rounded up all tapes of the event from all the cameras they could find. They were all classified and hidden away. Only 2 images were ever released which are grainy, blurry and after the fact. If there is nothing on those images then why after 15 years are they still classified? Does the intelligence service think that by classifying those tapes, the enemy won't know they hit the Pentagon? They don't want to show to some other third power the weakness involved in an attack up the headquarters of American military might? Or is it some other reason, as yet unexplained. So again where are those tapes?

5) Why? Why building 10 was pulled? It was not hit by a plane and fire should not have destroyed it. The response is that while not being struck by a plane the World Trade Center did fall around it and that might have weakened it. True enough. The why did the owner say the New York Fire Department told him they were going to pull it on a PBS special? And if the Fire Department did indeed pull the building, an

industry term for a controlled demolition, why could not that have been said upfront? Why the secrecy? Perhaps at the time, it might have been needed? I say again, after fifteen years, I think everyone knows that 9-11 was a "thing." So why was building 10 pulled down?

There you go. Five questions and nary a yo-yo out of place, a screw loose, or a full moon rising, just questions. All of them could be answered easily enough I think. For example question 4, on the location of all those tapes? They could answer it by simply releasing the tapes. Saying why they cannot release the tapes. But in the absence of a credible answer, the mind will fill in the gaps with conspiracies or phantasmal alien lizard me. For each of these questions we can only turn to government for answers. And that is no conspiracy theory either.

Gun Control

I was told with sincerity, after Australia confiscated all their guns, the crime rate soared for personal violence such as rape and murder. No gun to protect yourself and other people means that only criminals will have guns and the public at large is in danger for those animals. The thought occurred to me, that if there were no more guns then there would be no guns for a criminal to steal and then turn on people, so I explored the stats to find out that... dramatic pause clearly stolen from Monty Python "The Adventures of Ralph Mellish"... And nothing happened. Seriously, nothing happened. No spike in crime, No pile of dead bodies. Nothing. Could the same happen in the USA? Well why not study the matter. Oh wait. Sorry, The NRA allied with politicians to legally restrict all funding for anyone study gun crime and or gun violence. Why would they do that for? Well so they can pass off anecdotal evidence as their version of scientific fact. Gun owners are a single issue voter. Just tell them anything about guns that they feel is a threat and they will go nuts.

So what limited research we do have shows a lot of things but most of it bad news. So is there a correlation between gun laws and a lower crime rate? No. Why? Not all gun laws are equal. Just cause there is a law does not make it a good law, an effective law or an enforced law. So a straight count of the number of laws gives no clear indication. What about a reading of the law? Would that help the matter? No. That would allow in subjective criteria to play a role. What you see as being harsh, I see as lenient. In fact, we could list any number of possible criteria and they would all fail due to the same flaw of being subjective. All except one. There is a direct correlation in the number of guns around and their use. Make sense. If you do not have a gun, you cannot use a gun. For the most part, usage of guns is a crime of passion.

Whether it is to harm yourself or others, any time to reflect would drastically give different result. That would, in turn lower violence in all forms. Simply put, to lower gun violence and thus the number of mass shootings, simply make it harder and harder to the point of restricting gun ownership. The key problem being the NRA effectively targets anyone who dares stand up to them. Or at least they proclaim themselves to be that powerful. Imagine this, if 40 years ago the tobacco industry was able to outlaw research into smoking. Where would we be today? Everyone is smoking and people dropping dead from cancer and no one knowing why. Leading to perhaps the most incredible of conclusions; the tobacco industry is more ethical then the gun industry. How incredible is that? That or the gun lobby was smarter than tobacco in any case in their lobbying efforts. In America, it is so nice to know that people are being slaughtered in the name of gun industry profits. 90% of Americans want some greater form of background checks. The NRA says no. Thus the politicians say no. Best of all? You cannot sue a gun manufacturer for their actions in selling a gun as it is a legal product. So sayeth the congress, bought and paid for by the NRA.

Death Penalty

Look into their cold dead eyes of any killer and know this person needs to be put underground. That is why we have the death penalty, as a punishment for evil doers so they will never be able to do this again. So I would put to you this simple fact, death is an escape from any punishment that a killer may face. We are adding and abetting them in said escape. They don't care if they live or if they die. They don't care for your rules or societies concerns. They simply don't care. So we kill them and make us feel safer. Our prison system is supposed to be about reform. Well when dead you can deform, not reform. To reform, you must suffer. To suffer you must feel. To feel when you are dead inside is only possible with time, lots of time. The days grow weary upon the soul. Time passes endless and yet ceases not when the four walls close in on you. In maximum security, you only had time. Time to sit; time to wait and time to regret. In 1995 Oklahoma City bombing, Timothy McVeigh went to his death penalty smiling. After all, it was 168 to 1 with his death. He escaped punishment. All the state did was to take his life. Today some 22 years later, is he was still alive, he would be in the same cell, with the same walls, the same view, and same 1 hour of isolated outdoors he had the day before and the day before that. Now, if he had been left alive, he would be alone. Long since forgotten. Virtually ignored by all. And yet his mind would have all the time in the world to think of what he did. To think of what he accomplished in his slaughter of how many babies in that day care? There were 19 baby angels murdered by him. If no one else, they might have sparked a message in his heart. They might have invaded his dreams at night. They might have tormented him as his 'reward', punishment to any other way of thinking. Scrooge changed over night with but three ghosts. How many nights and how many of the 168 ghost would have haunted his nights? For this, we shall never know.

In 1972 at the Munich Olympics', Palestinian terrorist captured and killed 11 athletes. In the end three terrorist lived to tell their tale. While open to debate, they still fear the wraith of the Jewish State upon them. MOSSAD still hunts for them. Hunt being the right word. Now to be caught they having lived 45 years, they will die with much to lose and many more to regret their passing. When someone has death in their eyes, like those terrorists, or any child soldier they are dead within. You cannot hurt them or harm them. You cannot punish or reform. All you can do is kill them. With the passage of time, and the growing shadows of years, that death turns to life, and the fear of death creeps in with days. Then and only then, does time become the punishment itself. What waits upon the other side, if anything? Will it be seen as in favour of the slaughter of innocent? Or will it lead to an eternal torment and punishment to last all of the ages. We shall never know on this side of the vale, but rushing killers to the other side is not the answer. Let them live. Let them learn to fear that final trip. Let them know regret for their actions and finally let them understand the cruelest of all punishments is not to kill them, but to let them live in a cell for the rest of their days.

Privacy, the NSA and the internet

The NSA (National Security Agency) is reading your emails, and listening to your online Skype calls. In fact, they are searching and following you wherever you go online; to which ever site you are watching, reading or even playing on, right now. Even this one... Yikes! Invasion of my privacy scream the people. Conventional wisdom screams this is a violation of the American Bill of Rights, the Canadian Charter of Rights, my U.N. Charter of rights and every other rights guaranteed by various governments. Specifically the right privacy and unlawful search and seizure. They think is this a dastardly plan for world control! The logic of it goes like this; I send you a letter. So long as it has a proper address, postage and is sealed. It cannot be open or intercepted except by a legal court order, legally obtained. Otherwise, it is not lawfully held and people doping it can be arrested for acting outside the law in violation of so many statues that is it not funny; serious jail time and financial penalties. Similarly, if you plant outside my house, a video and audio surveillance camera, or CCTV type recording device that can film into my residence, in the absences of that magic protection, a court order, anything obtained is unusable and just plain creepy. And there is again all that notion of illegality, jail time and even lawsuits. A man or a woman's home is their castle and as such in inviolable except with the valid court order where then anything is permissible with the blessing of a judge. Ok with various nuances of jurisdictions, this is basically the way law works in a democratic country; certainly so in the United States and in Canada.

Following this logic, we turn to the Internet. When I send an electronic mail, email, it should be considered the same way as a snail mail letter. When I go online in the privacy of my own home, you need a warrant to see where I go, or listen to who I speaking with, just like as if you were planting a camera to spy inside my room. Ergo, the matter is solved, case law solves the mater for us and as such this is a closed book. They cannot do this except with a court order. Since there is no such thing as a global court order, all such activities by the NSA are illegal. And must cease and desist immediately. So why is it still going on?

Sadly the logic presented is incorrect. The fact that the law grind slowly but grinds finely is missing. They have yet to enter legal definition of modern technology for the most part. They are not sure if I sign a paper and fax it to you if that is the same force of law as if I signed it in front of you? Who uses faxes today anyways? They are so passé! When was the last time someone used a fax machine? Technology having outstripped the speed of law.

However, the law is not the problem in this case. In fact, the problem is our understanding of the internet. When I send an email it is not like a letter at all. A letter is a singular event. Going from one person's hands to another. In the case of an email, it goes to all parts of the internet to ask each one "Is this for you?" when it gets a no, it moves on. Your email stops when it gets to the right location. The government is able to read it and record it as it comes by without stopping it. Only someone with the resources of a government like the United States can do that, or rather can afford all the equipment to record it all to do that.

So one last thought, that super secret highly encrypted bank account information that was behind so many billion firewalls that it is not funny leading to your bank account? Oh yes that one? Well just as you are reading this on a web page, so too is your bank account. With the right guess you can land on that same bank account. While they code such pages not to be index by site like Google, those pages are as open as Google is, if you know the URL. So whatever you thought was private is not on the internet. Welcome to the modern world. Privacy does not exist. It is all in the area where you have no expectation of privacy. So to the NSA, who are reading this, carry on. It is perfectly legal to do so. Just as you are allowed to read my emails and listen in on Skype. I am not saying this is right, moral or even needed. However, it is legal.

Israeli Settlements

The Israeli settlement issue is against international law? Or so it is claimed. But is it? The first thing to understand is what is happening on the ground. In Israel, they are building housing for their growing population. Those units are being built on land that is of disputed ownership. As such, under UN resolution 446, 465, and the Fourth Geneva Convention, those settlements are illegal. Here is the law as it applies to the matter at hand and as such, black and white, those settlements are illegal. Plain and simple. Except you may have guessed Israel disagrees. So what? Who cares? They are biased and cannot be expected to have any other opinion. As such, they do not count. Except in international law, their opinion in fact does count. To bring the matter before the International courts, both sovereign states must agree to submit their dispute to the resolution of the International Court. Without the trial, all you have is presumed guilt. Without consent you have no trial. So to settle the matter, Israel is not violation anything international law has proclaimed for in fact no judgment has be issued.

However, by the same logic; Israel having a right to exist under the 1947 United Nations Partition Plan for Palestine has also been soundly ignored, not just by the Palestinians but the Arab world in general. In 2013 Hamas Prime Minister Ismail Haniyeh reiterated that the Palestinian Arabs will never recognize Israel's right to exist, nor any right to exist as the Jewish state. "Palestinians did not and will not recognize Israel." One can only then wonder why this point is not made by those claiming that Israel is violation of international law. Before one state can take another state to the international court, by overt action or explicit comment, they must acknowledge that the other has a right to exist, least there is no other party in which to bring suit against in any court.

You cannot sue a phantom, you cannot try a ghost. It must include real people, living in a real state that must have the real right to exist.

So no, there is no violation of any international, both by the lack of any such court case, any willingness to bring such a case to a court and lastly, any acknowledgment of the right of the other party to exist. Having said all this, we can thus go forward and say that this issue is a non-issue. The Israelis do not need to make settlements on those lands and should place them elsewhere. This is a lightning rod of for attention that need not necessarily be the case. It offers Israeli's enemies a soft target to attack that almost sounds legitimate. The real reason they make such settlements on contested land is to stick a thumb in the eyes of those same enemies, showing them, enraging them in some cases, that there is nothing that can be done to stop making those settlements. Until they listen to their better angels, the problem will continue the cycle of violence. The people of Israel and the state itself deserve better representation from their government. Simple as that, something choices are better than others.

Jian

A Sadomasochism abusive relationship where a bully tortures the submissive in a constant stream of physical suffering, belittling their intelligence, ability and any source of pride they may have ever had, but enough of CBC's programming cutbacks, I am here to talk about the Jian Ghomeshi being fired from the same CBC. When I first heard of he was on a break from his job, I was puzzled. First, I had to remember who he was, then to care a fig about his show, his programming or CBC. But then he was fired and while I was almost moved to care, almost. It turned out to be gas. But then, then! Jian posted his misses defending himself because he was fired for having sex. Which considering the prudish, puritanical behaviour of that corporation made so much more sense. Except, I still did not give a fig, fart or fluff. Even noted Green party Commandant Elizabeth May chimed in to support him. Could someone, anyone else have cared? With the sole exception of ex-Green Party deputy leader Georges Laraque whose very serious legal troubles actually registered on the who cares scale above both May and Ghomeshi for the briefest of seconds. This would be including his entire NHL hockey career such as it was. The whole drama it seems to me, aside from being purely Canadian and purely boring, was that anyone having sex at the CBC was to be fired. For the first clause of their contract to work there, is that anyone thinking of having fun was to be sufficient grounds for termination. Noting that they in fact had stolen the line from Ambrose Bierce's The Devil's Dictionary about Puritans "The haunting feeling that someone, somewhere, might be happy."

But then a miracle occurred. When the dark puritanical empire strikes back and release the kind of sex Ghomeshi was having. Not simply into spanking and light D&D. No this was outright brutality. Punches in faces were a turn on? Oh, ok then... Nothing even remotely hot about that. Or interesting. But the door was opened. And a producer was fast to tell her tale of how when she yawned in Ghomeshi's meeting once, rude much? He said some crudity that hurt her feelings. She alleged that he wanted to "hate f--k" her to wake her up," she says. I merely thought she had misheard being half asleep that would "Hate like f--k for her to wake up. Either or does not amount to much. I remember once, where a vice president in serious need of anger management lost it in a meeting and when on a yelling rant for 20 minutes. When he was done, he, himself, realised just how badly he had lost it and checked himself into anger management classes. (Come to think of it, he works at the CBC now. No sex please but screaming is allowed. Or is it?)Linden MacIntyre claims that being a bully is the norm at CBC indicating both Peter Mansbridge, CBC new anchor and the late Peter Gzowski are and were also bullies. As if being the final word was being a bully. It was their name on the show, so toughen up already.

The last note sounded in the sadly Canadian story of silliness when Toronto police arrested Ghomeshi for various criminal offences. And at least, it seemed that this story was indeed real. It was no longer merely the stuff of late night talk show host comedies. It had left from being the joke after Rob Ford to now being a legitimate news story and a criminal prosecution. Except for the massive media coverage. The mere fact, this was about sex and a legitimate Canadian superstar albeit on CBC and the media went all a flutter. Not nearly as much as Ford's own media circus but this was a legitimate news story no longer fit for the tabloids but real journalist could report on it now. Oh wait, after all this, I still don't care, So much to do about nothing

To be sure, criminal behaviour is illegal, Sexual assault should be reported to police immediately and being a jerk seems to be the norm at CBC along with its Puritanical over moralistic better than thou Goody Prynne behaviour. All of which is nothing new or even remotely interesting. Except in Canada, where the news media starved for anything to ever report is forced to report this as hard news. When at best fit only for the back pages of some low down, back alley scandal rag.

Jeff @ Amazon

An open letter to Jeff Bezos CEO of Amazon

Hi Jeff

Not happy here

My mother wanted some Danielle Steel books

So I help her out, she is not savvy on computers, I quickly open up to amazon.ca and start shopping

Bam right from the start

The search engine was crap

Had search in the category of books for I quote "Danielle Steel in books" in "the category of books", because anything else gets me a lot of authors whose name are not Danielle steel. It's like there are books and there are book-books but to search you really need to search in book-book-books....

So strike one.

But heck we went on. Usually you get good service....

Usually....

Not today

So I want on to search for her books. She likes to read books, so can I eliminate all the rest like hard covers and Kindle. Nope have to look at those because, hey, you have to push them on me. She does not buy them or read them but I guess the search engine feels they have to push that shit on her just in case no means maybe? Can I use the categories to eliminate those options?

Hell no.

No sophisticated enough...

Strike two

Keep on pushing forward to try and find something she wants...

Get her 10 books, mass market, ordered from all over the world... All those different sellers located around the world. Great stuff except for the price. See the price for the books was fine, but the shipping? That was cost 50% of the price of books. In the summary, before you buy is the total shipping price but there is no way to tell who is charging how much for shipping and handling. All I get is a large total. So I searched to eliminate those high costs... and what do I see... a large question mark going guess what? You have to look at the home page for each book otherwise it's a secret. So I could do that or...

After strike two comes?

You got it!

Strike three you're out!

Or rather I am.

So I went to Heather's site called Chapters Indigo

https://www.chapters.indigo.ca/

Canada's Biggest Bookstore: Buy Books, Toys, Electronics ...

www.chapters.indigo.ca

Shop Canada's biggest bookstore! Find bestselling books, toys, home décor, stationery, electronics & so much more! Plus get Free Shipping on orders over $25 or ...

A nice place.

Friendly, did not try to tell me I had to buy kindle, or anything else for that matter.

I started my search in books for the author and surprise all I got was the author and the books she wrote! And best of all? I could select the format I wanted them in! I then made a few more clicks and wow all I had was mass market books that my mother wanted. Wow and then when I went to order my books, I saw how much I was being charge for each one in shipping and handling. Why that would be zero not 50% of the total price. The books arrive on my door on Wednesday. Your orders would have arrived before April 20 for the distant sellers.

But I'll go you one further. See Jeff, I went looking to send feedback to the site. You know some weasel form you fill out that no one will bother to read. I found nothing on the site?

Why is that? Cause people are abusing it? Too many people saying they hate the lack of service? I don't know why, but I do not see a place where I could have sent this.

So strike four? Fourth down? Forced into your own end zone?

Now it was only a small order of 100$ or less, but it was still a hundred bucks I was willing to spend on your company that went to another web site because your search results are crap. Your web site pushes shit like kindle, when I don't want it and you refuse to accept that as a customer I am out to buy things that I want, not what you want to push at me. See Jeff, I am a simple buyer, I buy things I want, you sell thing that I want. Need meets greed and both come away happy. Can you guess by the tone of this email that *I* am not happy with Amazon? Sorry but next time, I will go to the other sites before you. You want to sell too much, too fast and too pushy. All the while not allowing me the chance to find what I want, how I want it and when I want it. Make it possible for me to buy what *I* want, how *I* want it and understand how much *I* am paying for each item. Not what you want to sell me, kindle, books by anyone other than who I want to search for and I want a simple bill that I don't have to do 8 million things to review. All on the order review page.

Is that too much to ask that you do the job you set out to do?

Sorry for the rant Jeff. I know Heather wants to thank you for drive traffic to her site. Maybe next time you may want to add to all those other things you are selling some customer service.

Diabetes

A single study shows that there is a link between diet soft drinks and Diabetes.

(http://care.diabetesjournals.org/content/32/4/688.full)

One explanation offered for this is a rather convoluted one that the gut bacteria are mutated by the soft drinks using artificial sweetener, aspartame as its means into rejecting sugar. Hence causing diabetes.

While I think the link is correct, the user or abusers of diet soft drinks do tend to get type 2 diabetes, the cause is far simpler than that.

When you drink a diet soda you think you are hydrating yourself as it is liquid.

In fact, diet drinks tend to dehydrate you. It is a diuretic, which means you need the bathroom more causing a net loss in water.

Studies show that people think that as it is "Diet"" you can take more and more because it is healthy. (This happens to all foods and drink labeled diet.)

*http://www.dailymail.co.uk/health/article-3137553/How-called-healthy-snacks-harm-good-People-eat-likely-overindulge-avoid-exercise.html)

So when you drink many diet drinks, you dehydrate yourself. And over the long term of excess use of diet drinks you create inside of yourself a long term state of dehydration.

Last link, dehydration causes an increase in blood sugar. Long term increases in blood sugar lead to Diabetes

Conclusion, long term dehydration cause damage to the body such as... Type 2 Diabetes. Therefore Diet drinks as the cause of dehydration can help cause Type 2 Diabetes even if there is no direct link top diet soda, but a link to the life style around it.

Champlain Bridge

First, one must better understand what passes as political cultural in Quebec. Montreal is an island. Surrounded by the Saint Lawrence River. As such, one must avoid this cleaning water and cross it to arrive in town. There are bridges and tunnels in place to do this. Now for the last generation, Montreal construction has been governed by corruption, collusion and downright theft of tax payer money in the form of bribery and kick backs that has been handed to a select gang of criminals. It is said that Montreal infrastructure cost price-wise 20% more and lasts 20% endurance-wise, less than similar infrastructure would cost in Ontario. The problem in part is twofold; first, pay off's, rip off's, political parties and their "Fund-raising" are all paid for out of the tax payer wallet and billed for already in the price of these construction contracts. The second issue is the lack of competition brought on by the near insurmountable government regulations designed specifically to keep foreign and other construction companies out of province. The simplest of regulation isolationism, can be seen in the demand that all correspondence be in French only. An American company might be able to do the job cheaper but will invest the time, money or energy to complete all regulatory requirements and do it in a foreign language.

The Champlain Bridge is the busiest express way in Canada with constant gridlock because it is overused by the population it serves as they head in and out of the island of Montreal. It is nearing its 53th year, having been built and completed in 1962. So it is in need of replacement. This is expected to cost 4-6 billion dollars. (Due to time and cost overruns, you can expect that price to double.) At the end, what will have happened? They will take a six lane bridge and replaced it with a new six lane bridge. It could not handle the traffic flow before they replaced it, so it will somehow be better able to better handle it when replaced by something better? You have grid lock with 6 lanes, and soon will have more gridlock on a new bridge with the same 6 lanes of span? And is this somehow anything better? Einstein's definition of insanity is to repeat the same experiment expecting different results. If you are going to spend this amount of money on a new construction using tax payer's money in the first place, then charge those same tax payer's a toll to cross on that bridge, why not think outside the box and build a bigger bridge that can handle more traffic and thus reduce congestion, serve the needs of tax payers using it and grant them service for their money?

This topic is rift with possible serious areas that need and demand people's attention and discussion, like cost oversight, the basic design itself and the question of tolls after. So then, what possibly could ever be more important than this topic? Why the federal government wanted to name the new bridge after local Quebec hockey star Rocket Richard. They were not going to rename the old structure just the new one, causing a hue and cry in the nationalist camp. Champlain, a man none of them even know anything about but he is a historical hero in Quebec, typical, names not substance politics, ignored universal 24/7-365 until some damn federalists tries to put up a new bridge and do not name it the old one. Sort of like, how dare U2 give away for free their new album? What an insult!

This passes for intelligent conversation in certain nationalist circles of Quebec. Ignoring the real issue, to focus yet again on breed and circus that distracts' tax payers from the government's boondoggle that will for the next 50 years force people into longer lines of commutes into town(Montreal), as the suburbs increase their population density and the bridge simple cannot, and will not handle the car traffic. Only now it is by design to not handle this traffic. Yet precisely because it is just built, no one will dare suggest they make a new one to relieve this pressure, for it works as intended. In other words, once the lobster is in the pot, they slowly turn up the heat until supper is done. In this case, the tax payer who pays the cost to get a sub standard build, based a substandard plan, created by substandard conservative government, based on some substandard thinking, aided and abetted by the local nationalist who could not be expected to see any of these issues as problems. After all, the area of Montreal 450 region, a belt around Montreal using the same single phone area code, is not the homes of the Pure Laine literally meaning pure wool, a term referring to the mythical founding Quebec fathers, who are still pure in thought and mind for the Quebec sovereignty movement. While often mistaken for third generation incest survivors who are only slightly deformed, ignoring the extra arm for flag waving no doubt and clear lack of vision or foresight beyond the end of their own nose, so who cares about them any ways.

This is what passes for politics in Quebec. Lots of heat but very little substance, only fit for bug eyed, bottom dwelling crustaceans also know as Quebec's tax payers. Who considering how high and how much they pay in federal and provincial taxes, clearly deserve better.

Pony Express

We head into the month of November, where we will soon be feasting upon the bounty of natures goodness freshly harvested from nature's bounty, while welcoming friends and family, from near and far off to celebrate and give thanks for blessings we have received. Those who cannot be here with us will still be missed but less so, for with a drop of an email or a video call they can be all but there for the meal and glad tidings to come. But overlooked in this plethora of thankfulness, we can find our staunch four legged friend, our faithful steeds, and our horses. The horse has played their part having assisted in the plentiful bounty, by first with the collar to pull the farm plow then to haul the harvest to market where we may purchase such goods. When not on farm duty, hitching the wagon or a sleigh to our friend would allow us to visit others, around the area which would have been the order of the day in the times not so long ago. Before the invention of the train or car, the fastest way to travel was upon our faithful stead! Galloping across land at in those days was seen as an incredible speed. Which when it came to sending messages across the United States, was first established using horses, called the Pony Express, in 1860 to 1861. In those 18 months of its operation, the running horses had reduced the time to send a message from coast to coast to a little over 10 days. A dramatic difference that soon would morph into the modern version of letter mail, the electronic mail or email that we communicate with today. So have a happy Thanksgiving. And pause to give thanks to our faithful steeds who play such a very important role in the feast with family and friends, present or not, never to be forgotten.

You Can't Get There From Here

Montreal is a most beautiful city. You may enjoy it, if you c can get out of the traffic jams. Seems that on every route, every bridge and every highway, there is construction, repairs or just imaginary things forgotten in the minds of engineers, waiting still to be called done, with the left over orange cones scatters about to mark the memories and nightmares of truckers, roadsters and travellers alike, who have to navigate the impossible rubric of a city transport grid run amuck. It is not just how much repair work is being done but how bad the planning of it is. On one particular bridge, they normally allow during rush hour in coming or outgoing traffic. So one day repairs needed to be done. So at 7 pm, when they switched to both ways, they blocked the out bound lane, where all the traffic was in order to repair on the side of the bridge. The inbound lane was opened to let in ten, fifteen cars. The outbound lane still had maybe 500 to a thousand cars wanting to get off island. But repairs come first. And that in bound traffic all ten of them had to be let in. The 1000 cars waiting were simply not important enough to consider. What is worse is that next year is the 375th birthday of Montreal. So the Mayor doubled down on construction and repairs to get in as much as he can this year, so next year will be relatively light on such things as needed in order to let the tourist enjoy the city. For all that, the bad planning, the traffic and the horrible drivers Montreal is known for, we are getting off lucky. Why do I say that? In the United States where they desperately need such infrastructure repairs. Where roads, bridges and highways are literally falling apart, they do not have the tax revenue to afford such things. In truth the bill could be as high as 4 trillion dollars at this point, and surely will go higher. But they have also a lack of will to tax their people in order to get the money to do those repairs. So whereas Montreal has a high rate of tax, as does Quebec, Canada too, the infrastructure is being renewed, repaired and rebuilt. Heavens knows what will happen down south as their cities, roads and bridges start to fall apart.

Teachers

Teachers can be petty, jealous and mean. The great ones inspire their students to soar above them, in skill and dreams to reach for the stars and chase comets across the sky. The worst merely try to tear their students down, like pulling the wing from an angel or a butterfly as if they were some tormented adolescent trying to rip the wings off flies. The best teachers fill us, their ever grateful students with the wonder and joy of learning, the love of the novel, the warmth of knowledge and the comforting friendship of thoughts yet to come, yet to be but always soon to become. The worst teachers batterer us with fear and loathing from their own weak, tepid insecurities that eke out their miserable existence trying to create more gloom dweller incapable of every learning to fly and be free of their own self-pity, contempt and disparaging existence. That is the sum total of our schools. For along that path lies every single teacher you will ever meet, from the good to the bad to the horrible. But just one caring teacher will change the perspective of that lucky student who will let them take off, and soar above it all, to reach out to become better than they are, above the petty fray of based meanness, drudgery, and mediocrity. The goal is to survive the bad teachers, ignore the incompetent, and embrace the greatness when you manage to stumble upon the few, the rare but always the best! Learn from those you can. Love those you will as for the rest, be they ever so humble, they are our teachers.

Thesis Evaluation

Thesis evaluation consist of an oral defense that is usually open to the public, this can has caused more than a few problems. Here are some of the worst nightmares that can happen. All are true stories. Here are my top five worst Thesis defense ever!

The first story was told to me by a professor as she was then a student. She wrote her PHD thesis in a year and submitted it to her adviser. The advisor read it and invited her to a nice restaurant for supper and then broke the news. "I am afraid this simply won't do." One year of work, flushed. So she went back to the writing table and rewrote it anew.

Another student when told took the opposite road and demanded a hearing of the full thesis defense board as is allowed by university thesis rules. They followed procedure to the letter. When the vote was cast, the student lost by a vote of five to zero. They failed him. And that failed him out of the program. So no Masters as a door prize as he left either.

A female student went to her defence where she had misquoted someone in her text; a very minor error that we all do. But most are caught in time before the defence. In her case, the problem was not the tiny error, it was the readers. Her advisor was hated in the department so they had one outside reader to be impartial and one reader who hated him. Well over this tiny error, the two started to go at each other. The chair asked the audience to leave. Whereas inside the shouting and screaming could be heard across the library as it went on for hours. Thirty minutes for her defence, and three hours of screaming. Degree earned, vote two to one.

When making enemies, do not piss off the vindictive graduate chair when planning to do your thesis defense, for there may be repercussions you have not considered. He first scheduled her defense in the schools largest auditorium, and then proceeded to order all the first year undergrads to attend this mandatory event. Then made sure a sign-in sheet was passed around. Normally you defend in a class room with a few people at most 20-30 people. She had to defend her thesis in front of 500 students who resented her taking up their free time. Talk about hostile environment.

Perhaps the worst thesis defense occurred for an international student who lived in Saudi Arabia. For some unknown reason she had to defend her thesis online and an Islamic religious policeman was to be in the same room as her. Now English was her second language so she struggled with it. The police officer spoke no English, requiring her to stop and explain to him in Arabic. If he got bored or if she took too long in her answer he would interrupt her. What should have been over and done within an hour at most went over near three hours. Where at one point he got up and almost smacked her. Only later would we find out what he was saying to her in the midst of her thesis defense. "Why are you doing this? You are just a stupid girl, you should not be talking to these men, you be fucking your husband so stop whoring yourself out to sound smart then you are stupid girl." She passed 5 to zero.

Bonus, a thesis on Foucault went seriously off the rails when the professor began to talk of this philosopher's sexual preferences, using non academic terms like "Fist fucking." He went off topic and spoke on that subject for near an hour before the chair could take over and call an end to the session.

Officer Paul Smith

I share this for information purposes and as a warning to people about scammers.

I received a call from "Officer Paul Smith" of the Canadian Revenue Agency. He got that far into his script before I hung up on him! How rude you might say! So why did I hang up on him? It's a provincial Holiday, so anyone calling from the government would not be calling here and never on a holiday. Second with my last name being French, they automatically assume I am French speaking and always speak to me in French not English. This officer called in English because he can only speak English. Our Governments are usually bilingual speaking both English and French. Lastly, this is an old scam. CRA only communicated by letter and email but never by a phone call. They are too easy to scam people.

This old con is where Scammers try to warn you about your impending doom, court cases, seizures and arrest should you not send them money instantly. And it must be sent now or they cannot help you with this problem and then bad things will happen to you. Being today is a Provincial holiday it would be very hard to find a place that is open to send money by Western Union. But again scammers don't know this as they are not even calling from the same country. They can pick up the money from Western Union anywhere in the world. CRA works by checks, bank drafts and gives you many weeks to pay any such bill, as does any western government. Scammers need you to run quickly in a panic and not think of it in any other way then presented. For it you did stop to think about it you would very much reconsider giving money over Western Union. I was watching something on the Large Hadron Collider and that is much more fun to watch than play with this jerk. So I just hung up on him. And yes I do know I am a geek watch such TV, your point being?

Ok, so a little while later the phone just rang again. It was from the same idiot "Officer Paul Smith" of the Canadian Revenue Agency only with a different voice. But the same name. The name is written into their script. If you can believe that. (Face palm) I said very loudly, "It's a scam, it's a scam!" The guy kept reading from his script as if that might mean something. So this is over and done with right? Wrong. I get a third and final call only this time it is not "Officer Paul Smith" of the Canadian Revenue Agency; it is an auto dialer with a recorded message from Canadian Revenue Agency telling me I have a problem that must be resolved by sending money yadda yadda yadda. I got online send all three numbers to the CRTC web site to complain about such scammers. It is a shame we do not have a way to contact police about such numbers. I once tried to do that with Bell and they have no way to block calls either. Worse, to report a crime you have to leave a name address and contact number as well as an email address online. I just want to report the crime, not get involved.

Anyways, if contacted by "Officer Paul Smith" of the Canadian Revenue Agency, just hang up the phone.

Professor Potter Lands a Muggle

In the distant but cold lands of Quebec, Professor Andrew Potter of McGill University wrote an article for Maclean's Magazine;

http://www.macleans.ca/news/canada/how-a-snowstorm-exposed-quebecs-real-problem-social-malaise/

Where he all but toss the province under a bus. In it he claimed; "Quebec is an almost pathologically alienated and low-trust society, deficient in many of the most basic forms of social capital that other Canadians take for granted." His evidence steams from the recent storm where hundreds of people where caught in traffic pile up on a major highway during a very nasty storm. Other evidence includes; "We're talking here about a place where some restaurants offer you two bills: one for if you're paying cash and another if you're paying by a more traceable mechanism." (Note the editorial change "Due to an editing error, a reference in an earlier version of this piece noted that "every restaurant" offered two bills. We have clarified this to say "some restaurants will offer you two bills.") And let us not forget: "Since 2014, municipal police across the province have worn pink, yellow, and red clownish camo pants as a protest against provincial pension reforms. They have also plastered their cruisers with stickers demanding "libre nego"—"free negotiations"—and in many cases the stickers actually cover up the police service logo." By way of conclusion, he writes; "And then a serious winter storm hits, and there is social breakdown at every stage. In the end, a few truckers refuse to let the towers move them off the highway, and there's no one in charge to force them to move. The road is blocked, hundreds of cars are abandoned, and some people spend the entire night in their cars, out of gas with no one coming to help. Forget bowling alone. In this instance, Quebecers were freezing, alone."

With respect Professor, I would suggest sticking with things you know, like that fantasy quidditch league you are in, or making up thing for Maclean's magazine to yet again slander Quebec.

Let's unpack this snowbound snow job and see just what happened. In a recent nasty snowstorm, Quebec was hit with huge amounts of snow, some place 70 cm worth and very high winds 140 kmph, which is a gale force range. So very nasty weather. It happens up here every winter. In this year's case it was also a perfect storm for government. Or more specifically, the traffic department. While the finger point is going on, it is clear the Transport minister and his department failed miserable to deal with this situation, but the problems can be spread around. Two trucks were stopped by the weather on a highway in Montreal. The tow truck arrived and the tow was declined. Why? If the trucker approve the tow, they have to pay, a fee of 2000$ was mentioned. That a lot of money for a guy making less than a 1000$ gross a week, if that. So what normally happens is Transport Quebec calls in the Provincial Police. They arrive, see there is a danger and order the tow. Since the police ordered the tow, the company pays for it not the driver. And everyone is happy. The QPP, as they are called, never showed up. The tow never happened, and the cars piled up. Now then where is the "Low trust" part of the argument? The truck drivers trusted the police to order the tow. Transport Quebec trusted the police to show up. The Police trusted that Transport Quebec would call them if there was a problem. But it gets better. The people stuck in cars began to call 911 to get help and were referred to the QPP. However, when it was notified at the city level that there was an emergency, because the fire department was called in to rescue people, the city sprang into action to help and assist those people. Through it all, where did most people stay? In their cars trusting one another to help, waiting, trusting that the state would come to help them, and trusting that they were safer waiting then risking the blizzard. Strange reaction for a bunch of low trusting people. Speaking of those police in clown costumes, it seems they were trusted to help as well. The police seemingly trust the population to not hold it against them they wear different coloured pants because they are protesting government contracts. Why, it seems that the police are also trusting in their Charter Rights to bring grievances to the government demanding redress in a peace manner, if but a riot of colours. In the end, the people were right, help did come, and after all, it was not the apocalypse. It was only a traffic jam on the highway in a snow storm. Both happen all too frequently in Montreal.

As for "Harry's" effort to bring in "Facts" (TM), Please note the trade mark for these "Fact" (TM), so not to be confused with alt facts or the more boring, plain and simple, normal facts. Potter writes; "Quebec isn't just at the lower end of a relatively narrow spectrum: rather, most of the country is bunched up, with Quebec as a significant outlier." To which any researcher would ask the pertinent question of; "So what, outliers happen?" There is a reason we do focus on outlier. We do not even consider them as part of the study. We report them and move on. For any number of reasons from poor translation, remember Quebec is French, to cultural shifts to simply bad sampling. In statistical research you expect there to be outliers, you do not make your research findings based on them. Sorry no points for Huff(ing) and Puff(ing).

My last point is to a much wider issue. What exactly is MacLean's problem with Quebec? Seems to me they try to sell as many copies on the back of a scandalous Quebec. No matter how wrong an opinion, how insulting or how wrong head they are, they never yet fail to print an article insulting Quebec. Only now armed with a Quisling, he teaches at McGill, and

McGill is in Quebec so he knows... As they pat themselves on the back for having done due diligence. Except they failed to be diligent or give the commentary its due, rather overdue, past due, and that it is really a Do-Do.

"Andrew Potter has resigned as director of McGill University's Institute for the Study of Canada, two days after writing a controversial Maclean's column..."

http://www.macleans.ca/news/canada/why-andrew-potter-lost-his-dream-job-at-mcgill/

This was his dream job? Insulting people, make false assertions and soiling the reputation of 6 million plus province? Cause we all eat at restaurants that give two bills? Professor Potter's next job will be with the American White House where he will investigate the Bowling Green Massacre, The Swedish Massacre; how the audience vanish at Trump inauguration, even though Sean Spicer say's it is the largest so it must be true, and he will be backing up Kelly Ann Conway by showing us how our microwaves can be turned into cameras that will spy in you. On second thought, best stick to the fantasy quidditch league, I hear tell you have Viktor Krum in your draft.

For more poems updated daily see:
https://poetoftruth.wordpress.com/